EAST

Leanne Kitchen & Antony Suvalko

EAST

Culinary adventures in
Southeast Asia

hardie grant books

Contents

THE
Southeast Asian
KITCHEN

Whenever we close our eyes, we imagine ourselves east. The word 'east' conjures languid memories for us. It's watching the sun slink into the Mekong and smelling the incense that wafts from every temple. It's the aroma of char drifting through city streets as restaurants stoke their embers for another night of barbecuing. It's the rhythmic thud of cooks pounding the freshest ingredients into fragrant curry pastes or a tangy serve of green papaya salad. It's the swish of saffron-hued monks' robes and the adventure that awaits in every row of street-food stalls. 'East' represents colour and clamour, chaos and calm; a place where traditions run deep – a vivid, stimulating, energetic and thrilling place, whose cultures and cuisines are never, ever dull.

Cambodia, Thailand, Indonesia, Laos, Malaysia and Vietnam – all incredibly distinct from each other culturally, ethnically and culinarily but, for us, together they are 'east'. In general terms, this book is our ode to all that we think of when we're not east and wish that we were.

We know we're not alone in being completely seduced by Southeast Asian flavours, and this book was born from our need to 'cook' ourselves back there, when the holiday was over and withdrawal symptoms set in. We might not always be able to perch on plastic stools and eat *banh mi* with Hanoi locals, or slurp bowls of rice porridge at shared tables in Java, but we've found that, through cooking, we can come at least *close* to reliving some of these treasured experiences. We've assembled a selection of the dishes that instantly transport us back to steamy, exotic, wonderful Southeast Asia – dishes zingy with fresh herbs and chilli, redolent with kaffir lime and lemongrass and pungent with shrimp paste and fish sauce; recipes punctuated with the crunch of peanuts, the soothing presence of rice noodles and the sweet richness of coconut milk; recipes where the cooking techniques are no more complicated than barbecuing, steaming, simmering, roasting and frying. All that's missing in these pages are the whiffs of a wet food market, the frantic blur of street life and the blare of Thai bubblegum pop tunes. Of course, feel free to adjust the balance of salty, sweet, sour and hot flavours in the recipes to suit your own palate, as well as seasoning with salt and pepper to taste.

This book is hardly exhaustive. It's a modest representation of the Southeast Asian culinary repertoire – entire tomes could be dedicated to the curries, noodle dishes or salads alone! Rather, we've compiled a selection of our favourites; recipes we find ourselves craving again and again. Some of these may be familiar, such as beef rendang, pad Thai or chicken laab. However, others are more esoteric – a sour curry of prawns and acacia leaf omelette could fit that bill, as might stuffed betel leaves with sticky tamarind dipping sauce. But cooking and eating should sometimes be an adventure, too. A trip to a local Asian greengrocer or supermarket to buy a few specific ingredients leads to all sorts of rewarding encounters, both edible and personal. If you come across any unfamiliar ingredients in the recipes, check the Glossary on page 266, where you will find helpful notes about the items and how and where you might find them.

For those who love Southeast Asia like we do, and constantly feel its unmistakable lure, we hope that, in some small way, this collection recreates its culinary enticements, without the need to buy yourself a plane ticket.

Basic Recipes

No matter what the cuisine, and regardless of the culture, good cooking relies on solid foundations. For Southeast Asian cooking that means curry pastes made from scratch; sauces, pickles and sambals whipped up using a few carefully chosen ingredients; and various types of rice cooked to tender perfection. None of these recipes is technically difficult, and most are not time consuming. However, the difference in flavour when you make your own, rather than rely on the store-bought alternatives, is simply out of this world.

Chicken stock

• MAKES ABOUT 3 LITRES (101 FL OZ/12 CUPS) •

Asian cuisines often use specific long-cooked stocks for various recipes, such as pho. But this is a good, simple, all-purpose stock that's handy to have on hand when the mood strikes for a quick soup or other stock-dependent dish. Use any chicken off-cuts or bones you want – although wings are cheap and give a really full-flavoured result. It freezes well.

3 kg (6 lb 10 oz) chicken wings
4 garlic cloves, bruised
8 spring onions (scallions), trimmed and bruised

Combine all the ingredients in a large stockpot. Add about 3.5 litres (118 fl oz/14 cups) water, or enough to just cover the bones. Bring slowly to a simmer over medium heat, skimming any impurities as they rise to the surface. Once the stock has started to simmer, reduce the heat to low. Cook for 2 hours at a gentle simmer, skimming the surface of fat and other impurities as they rise to the surface, adding a little more cold water if the water level becomes too low. Do not let it boil or the stock will become cloudy.

Remove from the heat and cool slightly. Strain into a large container, discarding the solids. Cool to room temperature then skim off any fat that has risen to the surface. The stock will keep refrigerated for 3–4 days, or frozen in zip-lock bags for up to 8 weeks.

Beef stock

• MAKES ABOUT 3 LITRES (101 FL OZ/12 CUPS) •

This stock isn't precisely Southeast Asian, but we often reach for it, as sometimes nothing but a decent, home-made beef stock will do. It's not hard to make but does require an eight-hour simmer. It's not worth the effort for less than the amounts given here – remember, though, that you can freeze any extra.

3.5 kg (7 lb 12 oz) meaty beef bones, sawn into pieces
    if very large (ask your butcher to do this)
5 onions, coarsely chopped
2 garlic bulbs, halved crossways
80 ml (2½ fl oz/⅓ cup) vegetable oil

Preheat the oven to 180°C (350°F). Put the bones and vegetables in a single layer in one large or two medium roasting dishes and drizzle over the oil. Roast for about 1 hour and 20 minutes, turning often, or until well browned all over. Transfer to a large stockpot and add 4 litres (135 fl oz/16 cups) water, or enough to just cover the bones. Bring slowly to a simmer over medium heat, skimming any impurities as they rise to the surface. Once the stock has started to simmer, reduce the heat to low. Cook for 8 hours at a gentle simmer, skimming the surface of fat and other impurities as they rise to the surface, adding a little more cold water if the water level becomes too low. Do not let it boil or the stock will become cloudy.

Remove from the heat and cool slightly. Strain into a large container, discarding the solids. Cool to room temperature then skim off any fat that has risen to the surface. The stock will keep refrigerated for 3–4 days, or frozen in zip-lock bags for up to 8 weeks.

Sweet chilli sauce

· MAKES ABOUT 250 ML (8½ FL OZ/1 CUP) ·

This sauce is incredibly easy to make and goes perfectly with barbecued meats, especially chicken and pork. Beware, though, as this stuff is way hotter than purchased sweet chilli sauce – you can vary the chilli amount according to taste.

75 g (2¾ oz) medium red chillies, chopped
2 garlic cloves, chopped
250 ml (8½ fl oz/1 cup) white vinegar
1 tablespoon fish sauce
250 g (9 oz) caster (superfine) sugar

Process the chillies and garlic in a food processor until a coarse paste forms. Alternatively, use a mortar and pestle. Transfer to a saucepan, add the vinegar, fish sauce and sugar and bring to a simmer over medium heat, stirring often until the sugar has dissolved. Reduce the heat to low and cook for about 50 minutes or until the mixture has thickened and reduced to a thick pouring consistency. Cool to room temperature. Sweet chilli sauce will keep, refrigerated, for up to 2 months.

Vinegar chilli sauce

· MAKES ABOUT 250 ML (8½ FL OZ/1 CUP) ·

In Thailand this is a common table condiment, added with abandon to noodle dishes in particular. It's called *prik nam som* and we like it drizzled over Five-spice pork (page 146), to cut the richness and add a kick of chilli heat.

8 medium red chillies, chopped
4 garlic cloves, chopped
1 teaspoon salt
170 ml (5½ fl oz/⅔ cup) clear rice vinegar
2 tablespoons caster (superfine) sugar

Cook the chillies in boiling water for 1 minute, then drain well and cool. Transfer the chillies, garlic and salt, to a small food processor and process until a smooth paste forms. Alternatively, use a mortar and pestle. Add the vinegar and sugar and stir until the sugar has dissolved. Vinegar chilli sauce will keep in the refrigerator for up to 2 weeks.

Seafood nam jim

· MAKES ABOUT 250 ML (8½ FL OZ/1 CUP) ·

With Thailand's incredibly expansive coastline, the Thai diet is rich in all kinds of fish and seafood, and much of this is cooked very, very simply. This dipping sauce is typical of the sour–spicy dips that make a perfect accompaniment for steamed or barbecued fish, lobster, crab, prawns (shrimp), scallops, clams (vongole) or squid. You choose!

6–8 green bird's eye chillies, thinly sliced
4 coriander (cilantro) roots, scrubbed and finely chopped
60 ml (2 fl oz/¼ cup) fish sauce
80 ml (2½ fl oz/⅓ cup) lime juice
2 garlic cloves, crushed
1 tablespoon shaved palm sugar (jaggery) or caster (superfine) sugar
1½ tablespoons chopped coriander (cilantro) leaves

Combine all the ingredients, except the coriander leaves, in a small bowl and stir until the sugar has dissolved. Stir through the coriander leaves. This dipping sauce is best consumed on the day it is made.

Nuoc cham

· MAKES ABOUT 250 ML (8½ FL OZ/1 CUP) ·

This is an essential condiment on the Vietnamese table and is used as a dip and a drizzle for a whole raft of dishes, including meat, seafood, noodles and rice. There are many different ways to prepare this, but we've opted for the sweeter, southern Vietnamese version (they love their sugar down south). However, feel free to play around a little with the ingredients to find what suits you best.

60 ml (2 fl oz/¼ cup) fish sauce
60 ml (2 fl oz/¼ cup) clear rice vinegar
2 tablespoons sugar
2 garlic cloves, finely chopped
1 red bird's eye chilli, finely chopped
2 tablespoons lime juice
½ carrot, cut into very fine matchsticks (optional)

Put the fish sauce, rice vinegar, sugar and 125 ml (4 fl oz/ ½ cup) water in a small saucepan over medium–low heat. Bring to a gentle simmer and stir until the sugar has dissolved. Remove from the heat and cool slightly. Add the garlic, chilli, lime juice and carrot, if using, and stir to mix well. Cool to room temperature. Nuoc cham is best consumed on the day it is made.

Soy bean dipping sauce

· **MAKES ABOUT 350 ML (12 FL OZ)** ·

Don't confuse the beans here for fermented black beans – they are an entirely different beast! This rich concoction is a simplified version of a recipe from Hue, Vietnam to serve with Hue pancakes (page 44). There they traditionally employ pork liver but we've left that out. They wouldn't be using peanut butter either, but it does make life simpler. You'll hardly feel cheated by the modifications though – this stuff is addictive.

4 garlic cloves, crushed
1 tablespoon vegetable oil
100 ml (3½ fl oz) hoisin sauce
2 tablespoons caster (superfine) sugar
3 teaspoons ruoc (Vietnamese shrimp sauce)
1 tablespoon fermented soy bean sauce or
    yellow bean sauce
90 g (3 oz/⅓ cup) smooth peanut butter
250 ml (8½ fl oz/1 cup) Chicken stock (page 14),
    or as needed
50 g (1¾ oz/⅓ cup) finely chopped roasted peanuts
2 red bird's eye chillies, finely chopped

In a small saucepan over medium–low heat, cook the garlic in the oil, stirring, for 3 minutes or until softened. Add the hoisin sauce, sugar, ruoc, fermented soy bean sauce and peanut butter and stir to combine well. Add the chicken stock and stir to mix well, then bring to a simmer. Remove from the heat, stir in the peanuts and cool to room temperature. Serve divided among individual dipping dishes, topped with the chopped chillies. This dipping sauce will keep, stored in an airtight container in the refrigerator, for up to 3 days.

Lime dressing

· **MAKES ABOUT 200 ML (7 FL OZ)** ·

This simple Thai-style dressing is wonderful poured over a steamed, whole snapper. You could also spoon this over steamed mussels, a platter of cooked, peeled prawns (shrimp), a simple seafood and watercress salad, or natural oysters in their half-shells.

8 coriander (cilantro) roots, scrubbed
3 garlic cloves, chopped
1 large red chilli, chopped
4–8 red bird's eye chillies, thinly sliced
60 ml (2 fl oz/¼ cup) lime juice
80 ml (2½ fl oz/⅓ cup) fish sauce
1 tablespoon shaved palm sugar (jaggery)

Combine the coriander roots, garlic and chilli in a small food processor and process until a paste forms. Alternatively, use a mortar and pestle. Transfer the mixture to a bowl, add the remaining ingredients and stir until the sugar has dissolved. Season with freshly ground black pepper. This lime dressing is best consumed on the day it is made.

Sambals

Sambals, widely used in Indonesian and Malaysian cooking, are a sauce (either chunky or smooth) or paste, served as a condiment with other dishes. They encompass a huge variety of flavours, ingredient combinations and cooking techniques. They can be raw, cooked (simmered, fried or deep-fried), fresh or preserved. There are sambals made using everything from fermented durian, chopped raw tomato and shredded green mango, to preserved mackerel and deep-fried dried anchovies. Generally chillies are a major feature of sambals and consequently most tend to be hot – some extremely so. These are just a few of our favourites but, really, an entire book could be written on the subject!

Chilli sambal

· MAKES ABOUT 250 G (9 OZ/1 CUP) ·

1 teaspoon trasi (Indonesian shrimp paste)
100 g (3½ oz) medium red chillies, seeded
20 red bird's eye chillies, seeded
10 red Asian shallots, chopped
6 garlic cloves, chopped
2 teaspoons caster (superfine) sugar
125 ml (4 fl oz/½ cup) vegetable oil
4 kaffir lime leaves, central vein removed,
   very finely sliced

Wrap the trasi in foil. Heat a small, heavy-based frying pan over medium heat, add the wrapped trasi then dry-fry for 2 minutes on each side, or until fragrant. Cool and unwrap.

Combine the trasi in a food processor with the chilli, shallots, garlic and sugar and process until a coarse paste forms. In a wok or frying pan over medium heat, cook the paste in the oil, stirring often, for about 5 minutes or until it turns darker and smells fragrant. Add the kaffir lime leaves and cook, stirring to combine well, for another 2 minutes or until you can smell the lime. Remove from the heat and cool to room temperature. The sambal will keep, stored in an airtight container in the refrigerator, for up to 1 month.

Lemongrass sambal

· MAKES ABOUT 250 G (9 OZ/1 CUP) ·

8 red Asian shallots, thinly sliced
4 garlic cloves, thinly sliced
6 red bird's eye chillies, thinly sliced
6 kaffir lime leaves, central vein removed,
   finely shredded
3 lemongrass stems, white part only, very thinly sliced
80 ml (2½ fl oz/⅓ cup) lime juice
1½ tablespoons shaved palm sugar (jaggery)
2½ tablespoons vegetable oil
sea salt

Combine all the ingredients, except the sea salt, in a bowl and toss to combine well and dissolve the sugar. Season to taste with the sea salt and some freshly ground black pepper. This sambal is best served immediately.

Tomato sambal

· **MAKES ABOUT 750 G (1 LB 11 OZ/3 CUPS)** ·

2 teaspoons belacan (Malaysian shrimp paste)
1 onion, finely chopped
8 garlic cloves, finely chopped
12 large red chillies, seeded and sliced
2 tablespoons vegetable oil
600 g (1 lb 5 oz) very ripe tomatoes, finely chopped
1 tablespoon sugar

Wrap the belacan in foil. Heat a small, heavy-based frying pan over medium heat, add the wrapped belacan then dry-fry for 2 minutes on each side, or until fragrant. Cool and unwrap.

In a saucepan over medium heat, cook the onion, garlic and chilli in the oil, stirring, for 4–5 minutes or until the onion has softened. Add the belacan, tomatoes and sugar and bring to a simmer. Cook, stirring often, for 30 minutes or until reduced and thickened.

Transfer to a food processor and process until a coarse paste forms. Season to taste with salt and freshly ground black pepper. Cool to room temperature. The sambal will keep, stored in an airtight container in the refrigerator, for up to 1 week.

Pineapple and cucumber sambal

· **MAKES ABOUT 750 G (1 LB 11 OZ/3 CUPS)** ·

2½ teaspoons belacan (Malaysian shrimp paste)
30 g (1 oz/¼ cup) dried shrimp
2 red bird's eye chillies
1½ tablespoons lime juice
1½ tablespoons rice vinegar
2 teaspoons sugar
½ small ripe pineapple, trimmed, peeled, cored and cut into 5 mm (¼ in) pieces
2 small Lebanese (short) cucumbers, cut into 5 mm (¼ in) pieces

---

Wrap the belacan in foil. Heat a small, heavy-based frying pan over medium heat, add the wrapped belacan then dry-fry for 2 minutes on each side, or until fragrant. Cool and unwrap.

Put the dried shrimp in an electric spice grinder and, using a pulsing action, process until finely chopped. Transfer to a food processor with the chillies and belacan and process until smooth. Transfer to a bowl and stir in the lime juice, rice vinegar and sugar. Add the pineapple and cucumber and stir to combine well. The sambal is best served immediately.

Sambal ikan bilis

· MAKES ABOUT 500 G (1 LB 2 OZ) 2 CUPS ·

1 teaspoon belacan (Malaysian shrimp paste)
1 tablespoon tamarind pulp
80 ml (2½ fl oz/⅓ cup) boiling water
90 g (3 oz/1 cup) dried anchovies
vegetable oil for deep-frying
10 large dried red chillies, chopped
6 red Asian shallots, chopped
3 garlic cloves, chopped
1 lemongrass stem, white part only, chopped
4 candlenuts, chopped
1½ tablespoons palm sugar (jaggery)

Wrap the belacan in foil. Heat a small, heavy-based frying pan over medium heat, add the wrapped belacan then dry-fry for 2 minutes on each side, or until fragrant. Cool and unwrap.

Combine the tamarind pulp with the boiling water in a bowl and stand for 20 minutes. Strain the mixture through a sieve, using your fingers to press down on the solids to extract as much liquid as possible. Discard the solids.

Rinse the dried anchovies well then pat dry using paper towel.

Heat enough oil for deep-frying in a wok until it reaches 180°C (350°F), or until a cube of bread turns golden in 15 seconds. Add the anchovies and cook for 3–4 minutes or until golden and crisp. Using a slotted spoon, transfer them to a plate lined with paper towel to drain any excess oil.

Combine the chillies, shallots, garlic, lemongrass, candlenuts and belacan in a food processor and process until a coarse paste forms. Alternatively, use a mortar and pestle.

Heat 2 tablespoons vegetable oil in a wok over medium heat, add the paste and cook, stirring, for 2 minutes or until fragrant. Add the tamarind liquid, 80 ml (2½ fl oz/⅓ cup) water and the palm sugar then bring to a simmer. Cook for 10 minutes or until the liquid has reduced and thickened, then stir in the fried anchovies. This accompaniment is best served on the day it is made.

Spring onion oil

· MAKES ABOUT 150 ML (5 FL OZ) ·

This handy garnish adds a burst of green and an incredible oniony flavour to Vietnamese dishes (noodles in particular). Although it keeps reasonably well, the lovely bright colour does fade on standing longer than a day, but the flavour in no way diminishes.

6 spring onions (scallions), trimmed and finely sliced
125 ml (4½ fl oz/½ cup) vegetable oil

In a wok over medium heat, cook the spring onion in the oil, stirring constantly, for about 1 minute or until the onion has softened. Remove from the heat and cool to room temperature. Use immediately or keep refrigerated for up to 7 days.

Chilli jam

What we know as 'chilli jam' the Thais call *nam prik pao*, and it's one of those incredible substances that can turn anything into a flavoursome meal. Used as a condiment with all sorts of dishes, it can also be used as an ingredient in soups, stir-fries and noodle dishes.

3 teaspoons tamarind pulp
60 ml (2 fl oz/¼ cup) boiling water
10 garlic cloves, finely chopped
125 ml (4 fl oz/½ cup) vegetable oil
6 red Asian shallots, finely chopped
8 large dried red chillies, chopped
80 g (2 ¾ oz/½ cup) dried shrimp
1 teaspoon gapi (Thai shrimp paste)
2½ tablespoons shaved palm sugar (jaggery)

Combine the tamarind pulp with the boiling water in a bowl and stand for 20 minutes. Strain the mixture through a sieve to extract as much liquid as possible. Discard the solids.

In a wok over medium heat, cook the garlic in the oil, stirring often, until light golden. Using a slotted spoon, transfer the garlic to a bowl, reserving the oil in the wok. Add the shallots to the wok and fry for 6 minutes or until golden, then transfer to the bowl with the garlic using a slotted spoon. Add the dried chillies to the oil and fry for 3 minutes or until they darken. Using a slotted spoon, transfer to the bowl with the garlic and shallots, reserving the oil in the wok.

Grind the dried shrimp in an electric spice grinder then combine with the gapi, cooled garlic, shallots and chillies in a food processor and process to a coarse paste.

Remove all but 60 ml (2 fl oz/¼ cup) of the oil from the wok and return to medium heat. Add the processed mixture to the wok with the sugar and tamarind liquid and stir to mix well. Cook, stirring, for 3–4 minutes or until very thick and fragrant. Remove from the heat and leave to cool. Chilli jam will keep in an airtight container in the refrigerator for up to 1 month.

Roasted coconut and peanuts

This is an Indonesian side dish or snack called *serundeng*, of which there are a few variations. Indonesians love crunchy elements in their dishes, using mixtures like this to add textural interest as well as another layer of flavour to their meals. Originally, *serundeng* was made using the squeezed, grated fresh coconut that had been used to make coconut milk – a savvy alternative to just throwing it away. Using thawed frozen coconut makes this a zip to whip up. Serve it scattered over an Indonesian curry with some steamed rice and plenty of chopped coriander (cilantro).

2 garlic cloves, crushed
1 teaspoon cumin seeds
2 teaspoons ground coriander
2½ tablespoons vegetable oil
300 g (10½ oz/3 cups) fresh grated or thawed frozen grated coconut (see page 28)
1 tablespoon shaved palm sugar (jaggery)
2½ tablespoons lime juice
100 g (3½ oz) roasted peanuts

In a frying pan over medium heat, cook the garlic, cumin seeds and coriander in the oil for 1–2 minutes, or until fragrant. Stir in the coconut, palm sugar, lime juice and 125 ml (4 fl oz/½ cup) water. Cook, stirring often, for 30–40 minutes or until all the water is absorbed. Reduce the heat to medium–low and cook, stirring occasionally, for 1–1½ hours or until the coconut is golden. Take care during the last 30 minutes, as the coconut can burn. Stir in the roasted peanuts and season to taste. This accompaniment will keep, stored in an airtight container at room temperature, for up to 10 days.

CURRY PASTES

Southeast Asia is home to so many different types of curries and their pastes, and including examples of them all is outside the scope of this book. However, these four pastes just had to be included. Hot and pungent Thai green curry paste, made with green chillies and kaffir lime leaves, goes well with fish, chicken and bitter vegetables. Thai red curry paste is fragrant with dashes of cumin, coriander, pepper, galangal and lime and laced with dried red chillies. It works particularly well with beef and duck. Yellow curries are a feature of southern Thai cooking and the paste gets its distinctive colour from the use of turmeric. It's brilliant with fish and seafood. Malaysian Nonya curry paste, with its complex spicing and chilli kick is a winner cooked with chicken.

Green curry paste

• MAKES ABOUT 250 G (9 OZ/1 CUP) •

1½ teaspoons cumin seeds

2 teaspoons coriander seeds

6 large green chillies, chopped

6 green bird's eye chillies, chopped

2 large red Asian shallots, chopped

4 garlic cloves, chopped

1 tablespoon finely chopped fresh galangal

2 lemongrass stems, white part only, chopped

5 large kaffir lime leaves, central vein removed, chopped

6 coriander (cilantro) roots, scrubbed and chopped

1 teaspoon ground white pepper

2 teaspoons gapi (Thai shrimp paste)

Combine the cumin and coriander seeds in a small, heavy-based frying pan over medium–low heat and toast, shaking the pan often, for 4 minutes or until fragrant. Cool. Transfer to an electric spice grinder and grind to a fine powder. Combine with the remaining ingredients in a food processor with 1 tablespoon water and process until a smooth paste forms, adding a little more water as necessary. Alternatively, use a mortar and pestle. The paste will keep in the refrigerator in an airtight container for up to 5 days. Freeze for up to 1 month.

Yellow curry paste

• MAKES ABOUT 310 G (11 OZ/1¼ CUPS) •

2 tablespoons chopped fresh ginger

1½ tablespoons chopped fresh turmeric or 1½ teaspoons ground turmeric

6 garlic cloves, chopped

2 lemongrass stems, white part only, chopped

2 large red Asian shallots, chopped

4 kaffir lime leaves, central vein removed, chopped

grated zest of 1 kaffir lime or 2 teaspoons finely grated lime zest

2 medium red chillies, chopped

Combine all the ingredients in a food processor and process until a smooth paste forms, adding a little water as necessary. Alternatively, use a mortar and pestle. The paste will keep in the refrigerator in an airtight container for up to 5 days. Freeze for up to 1 month.

Red curry paste

• **MAKES ABOUT 250 G (9 OZ/1 CUP)** •

1 teaspoon cumin seeds
1 tablespoon coriander seeds
16 dried red chillies, soaked in boiling water for
   30 minutes, drained
½ teaspoon freshly ground black pepper
8 coriander (cilantro) roots, scrubbed and chopped
8 garlic cloves, chopped
2 large red chillies, chopped
1 tablespoon fish sauce
6 bird's eye chillies, chopped
1 cm (½ in) piece fresh galangal, chopped
2 lemongrass stems, white part only, chopped
finely grated zest of 1 lime
2 large red Asian shallots, chopped
1½ teaspoons gapi (Thai shrimp paste)

In a small, heavy-based frying pan over medium–low heat, cook the cumin and coriander seeds, tossing the pan often, for 4 minutes or until fragrant. Cool. Grind to a fine powder in an electric spice grinder. Combine with the remaining ingredients in a food processor and process until smooth, adding a little water as necessary. Alternatively, use a mortar and pestle. The paste will keep in the refrigerator in an airtight container for up to 5 days. Freeze for up to 1 month.

Nonya curry paste

• **MAKES ABOUT 310 G (11 OZ/1¼ CUPS)** •

1 tablespoon belacan (Malaysian shrimp paste)
1 tablespoon coriander seeds
1½ teaspoons cumin seeds
1½ teaspoons fennel seeds
10 dried red chillies, soaked in boiling water
   for 30 minutes, drained
4 candlenuts, coarsely chopped
4 garlic cloves, coarsely chopped
5 large red Asian shallots, coarsely chopped
1 tablespoon chopped fresh turmeric or
   1 teaspoon ground turmeric
2 lemongrass stems, white part only, chopped

Wrap the belacan in foil. Heat a small, heavy-based frying pan over medium heat, add the wrapped belacan then dry-fry for 2 minutes on each side, or until fragrant. Cool and unwrap.

Combine the coriander, cumin and fennel seeds in a small, heavy-based frying pan over medium–low heat and dry-fry, shaking the pan often, for 4 minutes or until the spices are fragrant. Cool. Transfer to an electric spice grinder and process to a coarse powder.

Combine the ground spices in a food processor with the belacan and remaining ingredients and process until a smooth paste forms, adding a little water as necessary. Alternatively, use a mortar and pestle. The paste will keep in the refrigerator in an airtight container for up to 5 days. Freeze for up to 1 month.

Fried shallots

· **MAKES ABOUT 70 G (2½ OZ/1 CUP)** ·

These are a staple of many Southeast Asian cuisines and are readily available to purchase in Asian supermarkets. Generally the bought ones aren't bad and will suit most purposes well enough, but home-made ones will always be more delicious. Slice the shallots crossways and keep them moving in the oil so they cook evenly and all end up crisp. Don't throw out the oil either – cool it and re-use for general cooking purposes.

110 g (4 oz/1 cup) thinly sliced red Asian shallots
500 ml (17 fl oz/2 cups) vegetable oil

Put the shallot slices in a single layer on a clean tea (dish) towel and stand for 30 minutes to dry out a little.

Heat the oil in a wok or heavy-based frying pan until the temperature reaches 170°C (340°F) or a cube of bread turns golden in 20 seconds. Cook the shallot slices in the oil, stirring often so they cook evenly, for about 12 minutes or until deep golden. Take care near the end of cooking as they can easily burn.

Using a slotted spoon, transfer the shallots to a sieve to drain any excess oil. Transfer to a plate lined with paper towel to absorb as much remaining oil as possible. Cool, then transfer to an airtight container. Fried shallots will keep, at room temperature in an airtight container, for 1 week.

Pickled carrot

· **MAKES ABOUT 1 KG (2 LB 3 OZ/4½ CUPS)** ·

The Vietnamese are master picklers. They lightly brine a variety of vegetables and sour fruits and use them as ever-present accompaniments and condiments on the table. Cucumber, carrot, daikon mung bean sprouts and onion are typical candidates for pickling. Pickles are served with everything from *banh mi* to grills, dry noodle dishes and fried fish or chicken. These pickles are extremely quick to make although they do need two or so days for the flavour to develop.

600 g (1 lb 5 oz) carrots or 300 g (10½ oz) each carrots and daikon (white radish), peeled and cut into thick matchsticks
1½ teaspoons salt
115 g (4 oz/½ cup) caster (superfine) sugar
160 ml (5½ fl oz) white vinegar

Put the carrot in a bowl, scatter over the salt and stand for 20 minutes. Rinse the carrot, squeezing it gently to remove any excess water.

Pack the carrot into a 1.25 litre (42 fl oz/5 cup) capacity sterilised jar.

Combine the sugar and 300 ml (10 fl oz) water in a small saucepan over medium heat and stir until the sugar has dissolved. Add the white vinegar, then pour the mixture over the carrot in the jar. Seal, then leave to pickle for 2–3 days, turning the jar occasionally. This pickle will keep in the refrigerator for up to 3 weeks.

Cucumber pickles

· MAKES ABOUT 350 G (12½ OZ/2 CUPS) ·

Cucumbers are a refreshing presence in Southeast Asian cookery and are seldom put to better use than in Vietnamese-style pickles like this. These bracing, crunchy nuggets are the perfect foil for richer dishes like the Coconut fish cakes on page 37, or even spooned over a whole fried fish or grilled chicken.

60 ml (2 fl oz/¼ cup) clear rice vinegar
2 tablespoons boiling water
55 g (2 oz/¼ cup) caster (superfine) sugar
2 red bird's eye chillies, chopped
1 telegraph (long) cucumber, peeled and
  halved lengthways

Combine the rice vinegar, boiling water and sugar in a bowl and stir until the sugar has dissolved. Cool. Add the chopped chilli.

Remove the seeds from the cucumber using a teaspoon, then thinly slice the cucumber diagonally. Add to the vinegar mixture and stand for 1 hour before serving. Cucumber pickles are best served on the day they are made.

Vietnamese pickled onion

· MAKES ABOUT 310 G (11 OZ/1 CUP) ·

This easily concocted condiment isn't a pickle in the true sense. Rather, it's 'wilted' through the action of the sugar and vinegar. Sometimes we use it atop bowls of beef pho (noodle soup), but generally we make this to include in Vietnamese-style salads.

1 large onion, halved and very thinly sliced
125 ml (4 fl oz/½ cup) white vinegar
1½ teaspoons caster (superfine) sugar

Combine the onion, white vinegar and sugar in a bowl and stand for 20 minutes to pickle, tossing the onion occasionally. Drain well. Pickled onion is best served on the day it is made.

Grated fresh coconut

· YIELDS ABOUT 300G (10½ OZ/3 CUPS) GRATED COCONUT, DEPENDING ON SIZE OF COCONUT ·

Frozen grated or shredded coconut is hands-down the best convenience product on the planet, according to us. It saves so much time, is readily available from Asian supermarkets and doesn't cost a lot. Because you buy it frozen, it's easy to always have some on hand. However, if you prefer to grate your own, here's how to deal with a whole coconut, from go to whoa. Note you will need a mature nut, not a green one. And, although you can remove the meat from the opened coconut and grate the flesh using a box grater, it's easier to use a special hand-held coconut grater, which you can buy from Asian supermarkets. You can also buy hand-held shredders for long, thicker shreds. We tend to crack coconuts open by heating the nut in the oven but, if you prefer, you can whack the coconut in half using the back of a heavy cleaver, hitting it all the way around the middle of the coconut (its equator) until it breaks into two pieces.

Preheat the oven to 180°C (350°F). Using a screwdriver or something similar, pierce each of the three holes in the coconut then pour the coconut water into a bowl. Strain this and use it for cooking (it will freeze well). Bake the coconut in the oven for about 20 minutes or until the hard shell cracks. Remove it from the oven and cool slightly. Use a hammer to further crack the shell open and break the coconut in half. Using a hand coconut grating tool or shredder, scrape the meat from the coconut, taking care not to include any of the hard brown skin.

TO TOAST COCONUT

Preheat the oven to 180°C (350°F). Spread the grated or shredded coconut on a baking tray in a single layer. Cook for 8–10 minutes, stirring often so it cooks evenly, or until golden. Remove from the oven and cool. It will keep, stored in an airtight container in the refrigerator, for up to 2 days.

Sticky rice

· SERVES 4–6 ·

Sticky, or glutinous, rice is a staple of Laos and northern Thailand, where it is served with most meals. Commonly eaten with the fingers, it is formed into balls, which are used to scoop up small mouthfuls of laab and spicy dips and other concoctions, characteristic of those regions. Sticky rice is also widely used throughout Southeast Asia as a dessert ingredient. It has a distinctive flavour and texture, nothing like regular white or jasmine rice.

400 g (14 oz/2 cups) sticky (glutinous) rice

Put the rice in a bowl and add enough cold water to cover it generously. Soak the rice for at least 2 hours or overnight then drain well.

Line the perforated section of a steamer insert with a damp piece of muslin (cheesecloth) or tea (dish) towel, which covers the base of the insert and overhangs the sides. Put the rice in the muslin in an even layer, fold the muslin over the rice and set the insert over a saucepan of boiling water. Cover tightly and steam for 20 minutes or until the rice is tender – it will still be slightly chewy. Take care not to overcook or the rice will be soggy.

Turmeric sticky rice

Turmeric adds an unmistakable colour and a slightly musky flavour, while coconut just makes rich sticky rice even richer. This rice is a great foil for a super-hot sambal, such as Squid sambal on page 125. Leave out the turmeric if you like, but try not to skimp on the pandan leaves – the flavour they impart is dreamy.

450 g (1 lb/2¼ cups) sticky (glutinous) rice
1 teaspoon ground turmeric
3 pandan leaves, bruised and tied together in a knot
125 ml (4 fl oz/½ cup) coconut milk

Put the rice in a bowl with the turmeric and enough water to cover it. Leave overnight to soak, then drain the rice well.

Put the rice in a steamer lined with a tea (dish) towel. Add the pandan leaves, cover tightly and steam for 20 minutes or until the rice is tender.

Transfer to a bowl, discarding the pandan leaves. Using a large metal spoon, stir in the coconut milk and a pinch of salt. Serve immediately.

Pandan juice

Pandan is a flavour often used in Southeast Asian desserts. You can buy pandan essence from Asian supermarkets, in both clear and (somewhat lurid) green form. They're acceptable if fresh pandan leaves are not an option. However, the flavour, colour and aroma of fresh pandan is something else entirely. Making a concentrated extraction is as easy as chopping the pandan leaves and processing them with a little water, then straining. Simple. This recipe can easily be doubled.

12 pandan leaves

Wash the leaves well to get rid of any dirt. Drain well. Using a large, sharp knife or kitchen scissors, cut the leaves into small pieces.

Combine the leaves with 125 ml (4 fl oz/½ cup) water in a food processor and process until a coarse paste forms, stopping the machine every now and then to scrape down the side.

Transfer the mixture to a sieve lined with a piece of muslin (cheesecloth) or a clean tea (dish) towel placed over a bowl to collect the juices. Using your hands, draw the muslin into a tight ball and twist it hard to squeeze out as much liquid as possible. Discard the solids. Pandan juice will keep, stored in an airtight container in the refrigerator, for up to 2 days.

Snacks

For us, Asia is best described by the energy and bustle you'll always find on the streets – and the streets are always where the best dining possibilities lie. Grazing the day away on food-stall offerings, such as fish cakes and pickles, elegant sticks of smoky satay, flavour-bomb parcels of chewy-gooey-nutty Thai *miang*, or sticky pork and sago dumplings, is our ultimate pastime. Entire tomes could be dedicated to the diverse street-fare and regional snacks of Asia, but we've chosen a few personal favourites.

Miang

· SERVES 4–6 ·

Miang is a Thai street snack full of crunch, zing, heat and fresh-sweet-pungent-herbal flavours. The name loosely translates as 'food wrapped in leaves', and it's a dish designed to be downed in a single bite. Varieties abound – you can replace the peanuts with cashews, or add small pieces of tofu, crab, pomelo or shredded green mango. It's best assembled and eaten on the spot. Have everything cut up and in bowls, the sauce made and piles of leaves ready so diners can construct their own.

60 g (2 oz/½ cup) small dried shrimp, soaked in warm water for 30 minutes, drained and finely chopped

2 small limes, peeled and very finely chopped

100 g (3½ oz/1 cup) fresh grated or thawed frozen grated coconut, toasted (see page 28)

80 g (2¾ oz/½ cup) roasted unsalted peanuts, chopped

4 cm (1½ in) piece fresh ginger, finely chopped

400 g (14 oz) cooked school prawns (shrimp) or small prawns, peeled, deveined and finely chopped

5 red bird's eye chillies, thinly sliced

1 small red onion, finely chopped

2 bunches of betel leaves, wiped clean

SWEET TAMARIND SAUCE

1 tablespoon tamarind pulp

80 ml (2½ fl oz/⅓ cup) boiling water

1 teaspoon gapi (Thai shrimp paste)

4 red Asian shallots, finely chopped

1 tablespoon finely chopped fresh ginger

100 g (3½ oz/1 cup) fresh grated or thawed frozen grated coconut, toasted (see page 28)

135 g (5 oz/¾ cup) chopped palm sugar (jaggery)

For the sweet tamarind sauce, combine the tamarind pulp with the boiling water in a bowl and stand for 20 minutes. Strain the mixture through a sieve, using your fingers to press down on the solids to extract as much liquid as possible. Discard the solids.

Place the gapi, shallot, ginger and coconut in a food processor and process until finely chopped. Alternatively, use a mortar and pestle.

Transfer the mixture to a saucepan over medium–low heat with the tamarind liquid, palm sugar and 125 ml (4 fl oz/½ cup) water. Bring slowly to a simmer then cook for 25 minutes, stirring often, or until very reduced and jammy. Take care the mixture does

not burn as it reduces. Remove from the heat and cool to room temperature, transfer to a bowl and set aside.

Arrange the dried shrimp, lime, coconut, peanuts, ginger, prawns, chillies, onion and betel leaves in separate bowls or in piles on a large platter. Serve with the sweet tamarind sauce, allowing everyone to place a little sauce and the other chopped ingredients on a betel leaf.

See image on pages 30–31.

Steamed taro cake

· **MAKES 20 PIECES** ·

In its native Malaysia/Singapore, this dish is a very popular snack eaten in dining rooms and on many a street corner across the country. What elevates this snack to legendary status is the accompaniments – generous amounts of fried shallots, spring onions, red chillies and toasted sesame seeds.

50 g (1¾ oz) dried shrimp, soaked in warm water for 30 minutes
160 ml (5½ fl oz) vegetable oil
700 g (1 lb 9 oz) taro, peeled and cut into 1 cm (½ in) pieces
1 teaspoon five-spice powder
½ teaspoon salt
2 tablespoons light soy sauce
½ teaspoon ground white pepper
35 g (1¼ oz/½ cup) Fried shallots (see page 26)
850 ml (28½ fl oz) Chicken stock (see page 14)

200 g (7 oz) rice flour
8 dried Chinese mushrooms, soaked in boiling water for 30 minutes, drained and finely chopped

TOPPING

2 tablespoons toasted sesame seeds
2 spring onions (scallions), thinly sliced on a slight diagonal
1–2 long red chillies, thinly sliced
35 g (1¼ oz/½ cup) Fried shallots (see page 26)
small handful of chopped coriander (cilantro)

Drain the dried shrimp and pat dry on paper towel. Coarsely chop half the dried shrimp, reserving the remainder.

Lightly oil the base and sides of a 22 x 22 x 5 cm (8¾ x 8¾ x 2 in) baking dish.

Heat 2 tablespoons of the vegetable oil in a large wok over medium heat, add the taro and stir-fry for 4–5 minutes or until cooked through. Using a slotted spoon, transfer to a bowl, sprinkle with the five-spice powder and salt and toss to combine well.

Wipe the wok clean then pour in 2 more tablespoons of the oil. Increase the heat to medium–high, add the chopped dried shrimp and stir-fry for 2–3 minutes or until light golden and fragrant. Add the soy sauce and white pepper then add to the taro mixture with the fried shallots.

Bring a large saucepan of water, fitted with a steamer basket, to the boil over medium heat.

Combine 250 ml (8½ fl oz/1 cup) of the stock with the rice flour in a bowl, whisking until smooth. Bring the remaining stock to a simmer in the wok. Stirring constantly, add the rice flour mixture to the stock then cook over low heat for 4–5 minutes or until the mixture is thick and smooth. Add the taro mixture and mushrooms and stir to combine well. Spoon into the baking dish, smoothing the surface evenly. Steam for 35–40 minutes or until a skewer inserted into the middle comes out clean.

In the wok or a small saucepan over medium heat, fry the remaining dried shrimp in the remaining oil for 2–3 minutes or until golden and crisp. Using a slotted spoon, transfer to a plate lined with paper towel to drain any excess oil. Combine with the topping ingredients in a bowl then sprinkle over the cake. Cool the cake then cut into 20 pieces and serve.

Lor bak

· MAKES 24 ·

A Nonya favourite from Penang, *lor* refers to the dipping sauce and *bak* to the meat, typically pork but, for halal versions chicken is used. What never changes is the wallop of five-spice powder, which fragrances these crisp, meaty rolls. Traditionally associated with Chinese–Malaysian festivals, *lor bak* is an essential snacking item found all over Penang any time of year.

2 tablespoons plain (all-purpose) flour

80 g (2¾ oz) sheets of dried tofu skin

vegetable oil for deep-frying

FILLING

800 g (1 lb 12 oz) pork fillet (about 2 fillets), trimmed and cut into thin strips

200 g (7 oz) raw king or tiger prawns (shrimp), peeled, deveined and finely chopped

1½ teaspoons five-spice powder

2 tablespoons oyster sauce

1 tablespoon shaved palm sugar (jaggery)

2 tablespoons potato starch

3 teaspoons sesame oil

100 g (3½ oz) water chestnuts, finely chopped

1 small onion, finely chopped

1 egg, beaten

DIPPING SAUCE

150 ml (5 fl oz) plum sauce

2½ tablespoons lime juice

1 tablespoon caster (superfine) sugar

2 teaspoons tapioca starch or cornflour (cornstarch)

For the filling, combine the pork, prawn meat, five-spice powder, oyster sauce and palm sugar in a bowl and stir to combine well. Cover with plastic wrap and refrigerate for 3 hours or overnight.

Stir in the remaining ingredients and season well with sea salt and freshly ground black pepper. Set aside.

For the dipping sauce, combine the plum sauce, lime juice, sugar and 125 ml (4 fl oz/½ cup) water in a small saucepan over medium heat. Bring to a simmer, stirring occasionally.

Combine the tapioca starch with 2 tablespoons water in a small bowl and stir until a smooth paste forms. Stirring the sauce constantly, add it to the mixture in the saucepan. Cook, stirring, for 2 minutes or until it comes to the boil and thickens. Remove from the heat and cool.

Combine the plain flour in a small bowl with 2 tablespoons water and mix to form a smooth paste. Cut the tofu skin into 17 x 21 cm (6¾ x 8¼ in) pieces.

Fill a small bowl with cold water. Working with one piece at a time, lay a rectangle of tofu skin on a work surface. Dip your hand in the water and lightly rub the surface of the tofu skin with water to soften it a little. With a narrow end facing you, put 2 tablespoons of the filling, in a neat sausage about 9 cm (3½ in) long, along the edge. Fold the sides over the filling, then roll the tofu skin over the filling 2 or 3 times to form a log – don't roll it the whole length of the skin or the *lor bak* won't be crisp. Trim the excess skin then brush a little of the paste along the edge and press the edge to seal. Repeat with the remaining pieces of skin and filling.

Heat enough oil for deep-frying in a large wok until it reaches 180°C (350°F), or until a cube of bread turns golden in 15 seconds. Fry the rolls, in batches, for about 6 minutes, turning them occasionally so they colour evenly and are golden, crisp and the filling is cooked through. Drain well then transfer to paper towel briefly to drain any remaining oil. Serve hot with the dipping sauce.

Coconut fish cakes

· MAKES ABOUT 25 ·

These Javanese-style fish cakes are simple to prepare, easy to cook and packed with flavour. Any white-fleshed fish will work and, while we've gone for snapper, by all means substitute with what's freshest, sustainable and well priced at your fishmonger or supermarket. No chilli required here – just whip up a batch of cucumber pickles and you're away!

4 small red Asian shallots, chopped

2 garlic cloves, chopped

2 candlenuts, chopped

1.5 cm (½ in) piece fresh galangal, chopped

1 cm (½ in) piece fresh ginger, chopped

800 g (1 lb 12 oz) boneless, skinless snapper, john dory or any other white-fleshed fish fillets, cut into 5 cm (2 in) pieces

1½ teaspoons caster (superfine) sugar

200 g (7 oz/2 cups) fresh grated or thawed frozen grated coconut (see page 28)

2 eggs, lightly beaten

150 ml (5 fl oz) coconut milk

vegetable oil for deep-frying

Cucumber pickles (see page 27) to serve

Combine the shallots, garlic, candlenuts, galangal and ginger in a food processor and process until a paste forms. Alternatively, use a mortar and pestle. Add the fish fillets and process until the mixture is smooth.

Transfer to a bowl and add the remaining ingredients, except the oil and pickles, and season to taste with salt and freshly ground black pepper.

Heat enough oil for deep-frying in a large wok until it reaches 170°C (340°F), or until a cube of bread turns golden in 20 seconds.

Using your hands, form 2 tablespoonfuls of the mixture into balls then flatten into thick discs about 5–6 cm (2–2½ in) across.

Fry the fish cakes, in batches, for about 12 minutes, turning once, or until deep golden and cooked through. Take care when cooking as the cakes are delicate. Transfer to a plate lined with paper towel to drain any excess oil then serve them hot with the cucumber pickles.

Pork and sago dumplings

· **MAKES ABOUT 25** ·

Looking for all the world like jewels, and often sold sitting on trays lined with well-oiled banana leaves, the distinguishing feature of this Thai snack food is the exterior, made from a translucent skin based on sago. Called *sakoo sai moo*, they're delicious and fairly easy to make. Although on the streets of Thailand they make them tiny, ours are somewhat large in comparison. Just remember to wet your hands or the sago mix will stick madly to your skin.

2 large red Asian shallots, finely chopped
2 garlic cloves, crushed
1.5 cm (½ in) piece fresh ginger, finely chopped
1½ tablespoons vegetable oil
300 g (10½ oz) minced (ground) pork
1½ tablespoons fish sauce

2 teaspoons light soy sauce
1 tablespoon shaved palm sugar (jaggery)
½ teaspoon freshly ground black pepper
50 g (1¾ oz/⅓ cup) roasted unsalted peanuts, chopped
325 g (11½ oz/1⅔ cups) sago (tapioca) pearls
625 ml (21 fl oz/2½ cups) boiling water

In a large saucepan over medium heat, cook the shallots, garlic and ginger in the oil, stirring often, for 3 minutes or until light golden. Add the pork then cook, stirring to break up the meat, for 3 minutes or until the pork has changed colour. Add the fish sauce, soy sauce, palm sugar, pepper and 40 g (1½ oz/¼ cup) of the peanuts then cook, stirring, for 3–4 minutes or until the mixture is quite dry. Remove from the heat and cool.

Meanwhile, put the sago in a bowl, add the boiling water and stir to mix well. Stand until cool enough to handle.

With wet hands, take a slightly heaped tablespoonful of the sago mixture and form it into a 7 cm (2¾ in) disc in the palm of one hand. Put a heaped teaspoon of the pork mixture in the middle of the disc, then use your palm to cup the sago disc around the filling. Use the fingers of your other hand to bring the edges up over the filling to meet in the middle. Squeeze the edges together gently with your fingers to seal and form an enclosed ball. Put on a lightly oiled dinner plate, large enough to fit into a large bamboo steamer, leaving room between each ball for expansion. Repeat the process with the remaining sago mixture and filling – you will need more than one plate.

Put the dumplings in a large bamboo steamer in a wok or large saucepan filled with enough boiling water to come just to the base of the steamer. Put a plate of the balls in the steamer then cover and cook for 12–15 minutes or until the sago is soft and translucent. Scatter over the remaining peanuts and transfer to serving plates. Repeat with the remaining dumplings and serve.

Prawn and sweet potato fritters

· SERVES 4–6 AS A SNACK OR STARTER ·

Delicious *banh tom* originated in Hanoi, Vietnam – home to some pretty kick-arse street foods. As with many such dishes, versions abound, with some more battery, some more prawny and some with the sweet potato cut thicker. We like ours with a minimum of batter to glue everything together, and a ton of sweet potato and prawn. We prefer to use tiny, whole school prawns when they're in season but, if they aren't, or if you prefer, you can use small, peeled, raw king or tiger prawns if the crunch of shells and heads doesn't do it for you.

1 sweet potato (about 350 g/12½ oz), peeled and cut into thick matchsticks
75 g (2¾ oz/½ cup) plain (all-purpose) flour
90 g (2¾ oz/½ cup) rice flour
1 tablespoon cornflour (cornstarch)
½ teaspoon ground turmeric
½ teaspoon sea salt
½ teaspoon ground white pepper
300 g (10½ oz) raw school prawns (shrimp) or small prawns, peeled, deveined and sliced lengthways
vegetable oil for frying

DIPPING SAUCE

4 garlic cloves, crushed
2 red bird's eye chillies, thinly sliced
2 tablespoons white rice vinegar
60 ml (2 fl oz/¼ cup) fish sauce
2 tablespoons caster (superfine) sugar

TO SERVE

2 small handfuls of fresh herb leaves, such as mint, Vietnamese mint, Thai basil or coriander (cilantro)

For the dipping sauce, combine all the ingredients in a bowl with 190 ml (6½ fl oz/¾ cup) water and stir until the sugar has dissolved. Set aside.

Put the sweet potato in a bowl of iced water and stand for 1 hour to crisp. Drain well.

Combine the flours, turmeric, sea salt and white pepper in a large bowl, then slowly whisk in 225 ml (7½ fl oz) water to form a smooth batter. Add the prawns and sweet potato and stir gently to combine well.

Preheat the oven to 120°C (250°F).

Pour in enough oil to generously cover the base of a large non-stick frying pan set over medium–high heat. Drop heaped tablespoonfuls of the fritter mixture into the hot oil and flatten slightly with a spoon to form cakes about 5–6 cm (2–2½ in) across. Cook the fritters, in batches, for 3 minutes on each side, or until deep golden and the prawns and sweet potato are cooked through.

Drain the fritters on paper towel and keep them warm in the oven until all the fritters are cooked.

Serve the fritters with the herbs scattered over and the dipping sauce, passed separately.

Hue pancakes

· **MAKES 6** ·

In Hue, Vietnam, these pancakes are known as *banh khoai*, which translates as 'happy cake', and happiness is certainly what you'll experience when you master this classic street dish. The key to replicating it at home is to get your frying pan nice and hot and to spread an even layer of the batter across the pan – this helps make the pancake crisp and the crisper these are, the better they are.

vegetable oil for cooking

2 eggs, beaten

200 g (7 oz) cooked school prawns (shrimp)

200 g (7 oz) Chinese barbecued pork (char siu) (available from Asian barbecue shops), thinly sliced

3 spring onions (scallions), thinly sliced

250 g (9 oz) bean sprouts

1 bunch of perilla leaves

1 bunch of mint leaves

1 bunch of Vietnamese mint leaves

BATTER

130 g (¾ cup) rice flour

½ teaspoon ground turmeric

1 egg, lightly beaten

1 teaspoon caster (superfine) sugar

100 ml (3½ fl oz) coconut cream

½ teaspoon salt

TO SERVE

butter lettuce leaves

Soy bean dipping sauce (see page 17)

To make the batter, combine all the ingredients in a bowl with 150 ml (5 fl oz) cold water and whisk until a smooth, creamy batter forms with the consistency of pouring (single/light) cream. Add a little extra water if necessary.

Heat 1 tablespoon oil in a 20 cm (8 in) heavy-based frying pan over high heat. Add 60 ml (2 fl oz/¼ cup) of the batter to the pan, swirling the pan to coat the base evenly. Add about one-sixth of the beaten egg, then one-sixth of the prawns, barbecued pork, spring onion, bean sprouts and herbs. Cook for 2 minutes or until the base is crisp and golden and the pancake is cooked through. Fold over, transfer to a plate and cover with foil to keep warm. Repeat the process with the remaining batter and filling ingredients.

Serve the pancakes with the lettuce and the soy bean dipping sauce on the side.

MIXED VEGETABLES AND DIPS

· SERVES 6 ·

We think that serving a Southeast Asian crudité platter is a truly fabulous way to get your greens. You can be wild and loose with the variety and amount of vegetables in this recipe, so substitute your favourites or go with what's in season. Or, for a change, try blanching some bitter melon, cutting carrots into chunky batons or using slices of green papaya. There's enough going on here to crack open a Singha, sit outside and start planning your next Asian holiday!

about 200 g (7 oz) each of raw cabbage, snake (yard-long) beans, apple eggplant (aubergine), cucumber, wing beans or other vegetables of your choice
rice crackers to serve (optional)

Yellow bean dip

150 g (5½ oz) minced (ground) pork
2 teaspoons vegetable oil
250 ml (8½ fl oz/1 cup) coconut milk
150 g (5½ oz/½ cup) yellow bean sauce, mashed
3 red Asian shallots, very finely chopped
2 tablespoons lime juice
3 teaspoons caster (superfine) sugar
1 tablespoon fish sauce
2 red bird's eye chillies, thinly sliced, plus extra to garnish

---

In a wok over medium heat, cook the pork in the oil for 2–3 minutes. Add the coconut milk and yellow bean sauce and stir to combine well. Add the remaining ingredients and simmer for 8–10 minutes or until the mixture reduces slightly and thickens. Season to taste with salt and freshly ground black pepper then serve warm, garnished with the extra sliced chilli, with the vegetables for dipping.

Eggplant dip

6 dried red chillies, chopped
4 small red Asian shallots, coarsely chopped
4 garlic cloves, coarsely chopped
60 ml (2 fl oz/¼ cup) vegetable oil
2 teaspoons tamarind pulp
2 tablespoons boiling water
800 g (1 lb 12 oz) Japanese eggplants (aubergines)
1½ tablespoons shaved palm sugar (jaggery)
1 tablespoon fish sauce
2½ tablespoons lime juice
2 spring onions (scallions), finely chopped
handful of coriander (cilantro), chopped

Dry-fry the chillies for 5–7 minutes in a frying pan over medium heat. Transfer to a bowl. Increase the heat to medium–high and dry-fry the shallots and garlic for 6–8 minutes. Process in a food processor with the chillies until a coarse paste forms, gradually adding half the oil. In a wok over medium heat, cook the paste in the remaining oil for 2 minutes or until fragrant. Remove from the heat.

Combine the tamarind pulp with the boiling water in a small bowl and stand for 20 minutes. Strain the mixture through a sieve, using your fingers to press down on the solids to extract as much liquid as possible. Discard the solids.

Cook the eggplants over a gas flame, turning often, for 8–10 minutes until blackened and soft. Transfer to a bowl. When cool, peel and transfer to a food processor with the palm sugar, fish sauce, lime juice, tamarind liquid and cooked paste. Pulse until a coarse paste forms. Season, stir in the spring onions and coriander and serve with the vegetables for dipping.

SATAYS

· **SERVES 4–6** ·

It's believed that satay, or sate, was invented by Javanese street vendors and was based on the Indian kebab, brought to Indonesia by Muslim traders. We've chosen two popular types – lamb and chicken, and prepared them local-style, small and dainty! The best way to cook these is the Javanese way, over coals, but a barbecue will do just as well. Be careful to char, and not burn. Serve with simple steamed rice.

Lamb satay

3 teaspoons coriander seeds

150 ml (5 fl oz) kecap manis

2 garlic cloves, crushed

½ teaspoon ground white pepper

1½ tablespoons lime juice

1 kg (2 lb 3 oz) boneless lamb leg, excess fat trimmed and cut into 1.5 cm (½ in) pieces

30 wooden skewers, soaked in water for 30 minutes

4 small red Asian shallots, finely chopped

thinly sliced red bird's eye chilli to garnish

rice crackers to serve

Heat a heavy-based frying pan over medium–low heat, add the coriander seeds and dry-fry for 3 minutes or until fragrant. Grind to a fine powder in an electric spice grinder.

Transfer the ground coriander to a bowl and combine with the kecap manis, garlic, white pepper and lime juice.

Thread 3 pieces of lamb onto each skewer and season with salt and pepper. Lightly brush each skewer with the kecap manis mixture. Reserve any mixture, combine it with the shallots and set aside.

Heat a barbecue or chargrill pan to medium–high and cook the satay skewers, in batches if necessary, turning often, for 6–8 minutes or until cooked through. Serve garnished with the sliced chilli, the reserved kecap manis mixture for dipping and a few rice crackers.

Chicken satay

1 kg (2 lb 3 oz) boneless, skinless chicken thighs, trimmed and cut into 1.5 cm (½ in) pieces

30 wooden skewers, soaked in water for 30 minutes

PASTE

2 lemongrass stems, white part only, chopped

8 kaffir lime leaves, central vein removed, chopped

1 tablespoon chopped fresh galangal

2 garlic cloves, crushed

2 teaspoons ground turmeric

2½ tablespoons light soy sauce

2½ tablespoons shaved palm sugar (jaggery)

2½ tablespoons vegetable oil

For the paste, combine all the ingredients in a food processor and process until a smooth paste forms. Combine the paste with the chicken in a bowl, using your hands to coat the chicken well. Cover with plastic wrap and refrigerate overnight.

Before cooking, remove the chicken from the marinade, reserving the marinade.

Heat a barbecue or chargrill pan to medium–high. Thread 3 pieces of chicken onto each skewer and season to taste with salt and pepper. Cook the chicken, in batches if necessary, turning and brushing with the reserved marinade from time to time, for 6–8 minutes or until cooked through. Serve with lime wedges for squeezing over.

Coconut beef patties

· SERVES 6 ·

In Vietnam, patties like this are called *cha bo* and tend to have a somewhat bouncy texture. We also love the Laotian charcoal-grilled pork patties, which you find in the atmospheric food market in the Old Town part of Luang Prabang, made using minced (ground) pork, flavoured with shallots, lemongrass and pepper. This recipe draws on elements of both to make these versatile meaty bites. Use pork mince if you prefer and stuff the mixture into baguettes with pickled carrot, mayonnaise, maybe a layer of pâté and plenty of herb leaves (mint, Vietnamese mint and coriander).

BEEF PATTIES

5 garlic cloves, coarsely chopped

3 large red Asian shallots, coarsely chopped

110 g (4 oz/⅔ cup) roasted, unsalted peanuts

800 g (1 lb 12 oz) minced (ground) beef

125 ml (4 fl oz/½ cup) thick coconut milk

1½ tablespoons fish sauce

1 tablespoon caster (superfine) sugar

1½ teaspoons salt

2 teaspoons freshly ground black pepper

vegetable oil for brushing

TO SERVE

21.5 cm (8½ inch) round dried rice paper wrappers

1 butter lettuce, leaves washed, dried and torn into large pieces

250 g (9 oz) cooked thin fresh rice noodles

Pickled carrot using half carrot and half daikon (white radish) (see page 26)

coriander (cilantro), Thai basil, perilla leaves and mint sprigs

Sriracha sauce and Hoisin sauce for dipping

For the beef patties, combine the garlic and shallots in a food processor and pulse to chop coarsely. Add the peanuts and process until everything is quite finely chopped. Add the beef, coconut milk, fish sauce, sugar, salt and pepper and process until the mixture is smooth and a little elastic.

Line a large tray with baking paper.

Take small handfuls of the beef mixture and use your hands to roll them into balls. Flatten each one to a round about 6 cm (2½ in) across, and place on the tray. Continue until all the mixture has been made into patties.

Heat a chargrill pan or a large, heavy-based frying pan over medium heat. Brush one side of the patties lightly with oil then cook, in batches, oiled side down, for 4–5 minutes, turning once, or until lightly charred and cooked through.

Serve the patties on a large, warmed platter with the remaining ingredients in bowls and with individual bowls of warm water for diners to dip and soften the rice paper wrappers. Let everyone assemble their own wrappers, placing torn pieces of the patties, lettuce, noodles, pickles and herbs in each, then rolling up and dipping in your sauce of choice before eating.

Soups

Throughout Southeast Asia, soups form such a crucial part of the culinary repertoire, that it would be remiss to not include a few in this book. Narrowing down all those myriad lush, brothy, noodle-y, meaty, chilli-fied variations to a handful of all-time favourites is definitely a tough call. However, here are the soups that we find ourselves cooking, time and time again, from a simple Vietnamese-inspired noodle soup made using ready-cooked duck, to a complex and satisfying bowl of laksa.

Laksa

· **SERVES 4** ·

We all know (and love) laksa, which originated with the Nonyas in Malaysia. The classic laksa, recreated here, is curry laksa, or *laksa lemak*, and is coconut milk–based. The celebrated *asam laksa*, which has no coconut cream, is fish-based with lovely light, sour, herbal flavours. We love *asam laksa*, but it's pretty difficult to recreate at home. No matter, as this one is a winner too.

60 ml (2 fl oz/¼ cup) vegetable oil

1.5 litres (51 fl oz/6 cups) Chicken stock (see page 14)

2½ teaspoons grated palm sugar (jaggery)

450 g (1 lb) chicken thighs with bone and skin, or boneless, skinless chicken thighs, thickly sliced

12 medium raw king prawns (shrimp), shelled and deveined, tails left intact

500 ml (17 fl oz/2 cups) coconut milk

12 store-bought fish balls (available from Asian supermarkets)

150 g (5½ oz) tofu puffs, thickly sliced (available from Asian supermarkets)

200 g (7 oz) bean sprouts plus extra to garnish

500 g (1 lb 2 oz) fresh thin rice noodles

LAKSA PASTE

1 tablespoon belacan (Malaysian shrimp paste)

8 small dried red chillies, soaked in boiling water for 30 minutes, drained

2 tablespoons dried shrimp, soaked in warm water for 30 minutes, drained

5 red Asian shallots, chopped

1 tablespoon finely chopped fresh galangal

3 garlic cloves, chopped

2 large lemongrass stems, white part only, chopped

6 candlenuts, chopped

2 teaspoons ground coriander

1 teaspoon sweet paprika

1 teaspoon ground cumin

1 teaspoon ground turmeric

TO SERVE

Fried shallots (see page 26)

Vietnamese mint leaves

Chilli sambal (see page 18) (optional)

lime wedges

For the paste, wrap the belacan in foil. Heat a small, heavy-based frying pan over medium heat, add the wrapped belacan then dry-fry for 2 minutes on each side, or until fragrant. Cool and unwrap.

Combine the belacan and the remaining paste ingredients in a food processor and process to a smooth paste. Alternatively, use a mortar and pestle.

In a large saucepan over medium heat, cook the laksa paste in the oil, stirring, for 2 minutes or until fragrant. Add the stock and sugar. Stir to combine, then bring to a simmer. Add the chicken, return to a simmer and cook for 4 minutes. Add the prawns and cook for 1 minute or until the chicken is cooked through and the prawns are almost cooked. Add the coconut milk, fish balls, tofu puffs and bean sprouts. Stir gently to combine, then bring almost to a simmer. Reduce the heat to low and cook for 2 minutes or until the prawns are just cooked, the bean sprouts are wilted and the fish balls and tofu are heated through.

Meanwhile, put the noodles in a large bowl. Pour over enough boiling water to cover and stand for 2 minutes or until heated through. Drain well. Divide the noodles among serving bowls and top with the laksa mixture. Scatter over the fried shallots, mint leaves and extra bean sprouts. Spoon over the chilli sambal, if using, and serve immediately with the lime wedges.

See image on pages 54–55.

Coconut noodle soup

· **SERVES 6** ·

Called *ohn-no-khakswe* by the Burmese – *ohn-no* being coconut and *khakswe* meaning noodles – this dish is worthy of the title Asian fusion. Fusion cooking can – to us anyway– seem contrived, but here the ingredients are a nod to Burma's geography, neighbours and history. There's ginger, turmeric and besan from India, coconut milk from Thailand and the Chinese influence of wok cooking.

900 g (2 lb) boneless, skinless chicken thighs (about 6 in total)

1½ teaspoons salt

1 teaspoon ground turmeric

2 tablespoons fish sauce, plus extra to taste

4 garlic cloves, crushed

4 small dried red chillies, soaked in boiling water for 30 minutes, drained

2.5 cm (1 in) piece fresh ginger, chopped

2 large onions, thinly sliced

60 ml (2 fl oz/¼ cup) vegetable oil

2 teaspoons hot paprika

1.25 litres (42 fl oz/5 cups) Chicken stock (see page 14)

30 g (1 oz/¼ cup) besan (chickpea flour)

400 ml (14 fl oz) coconut milk

TO SERVE

500 g (1 lb 2 oz) cooked fresh egg noodles

lime wedges

4 hard-boiled eggs, peeled and cut into wedges

dried chilli flakes

1 small onion, very thinly sliced

fried noodles (available from Asian supermarkets)

coriander (cilantro) leaves

Combine the chicken, salt, turmeric and fish sauce in a bowl and use your hands to combine well. Stand for 30 minutes at cool room temperature.

Combine the garlic, dried chillies and ginger in a food processor and process until a smooth paste forms. Alternatively, use a mortar and pestle.

In a large saucepan over medium heat, cook the onion in half the oil, stirring often, for 15 minutes or until the onion is golden.

Meanwhile, in a large non-stick frying pan over medium heat, cook the chicken, paste and paprika in the remaining oil, stirring, for 5–7 minutes or until the chicken changes colour all over. Season well with freshly ground black pepper. Add to the onion in the pan with all but 60 ml (2 fl oz/¼ cup) of the chicken stock.

Combine the reserved stock in a bowl with the besan, mixing to form a smooth paste.

Bring the stock in the pan to a simmer then add the flour paste and stir until the mixture returns to a simmer. Cook for 8–10 minutes, stirring occasionally to prevent lumps forming, or until the chicken is cooked through, adding a little extra fish sauce to taste if desired. Add the coconut milk and cook just until it is about to simmer, to heat it through.

To serve, divide the cooked egg noodles among large bowls then ladle the curry mixture over. Serve with the lime wedges, eggs, chilli flakes, thinly sliced onion, fried noodles and coriander.

Duck and egg noodle soup

· **SERVES 6** ·

There's a huge Chinese influence on Vietnamese cuisine, which is maybe why, as avowed Sinophiles, we love it so much. The ingredients in this dish are pure Chinese, spiked with the unmistakably Vietnamese touches of fish sauce, palm sugar and a scattering of dried chillies. This easy recreation of a Saigon classic uses cooked duck from an Asian barbecue shop. However, if you prefer, you could marinate raw duck leg quarters in dark soy, sugar and garlic, then simmer in the stock with the spices for an hour or until the meat is tender, then proceed with the recipe as below.

1.5 litres (51 fl oz/6 cups) Chicken stock (see page 14)

1 cinnamon stick

2 star anise

6 whole cloves

6 dried red chillies

4 cm (1½ in) piece fresh ginger, cut into fine matchsticks

3 garlic cloves, bruised

18 dried shiitake mushrooms, soaked in boiling water for 30 minutes, drained

60 ml (2 fl oz/¼ cup) fish sauce

2 tablespoons light soy sauce

3 teaspoons dark soy sauce

1 tablespoon shaved palm sugar (jaggery)

2 bunches of choy sum

500 g (1 lb 2 oz) thin fresh egg noodles

1½ Chinese barbecued ducks, cut into 6 pieces (available from Asian barbecue shops – ask them to cut it up for you)

small handful coriander (cilantro), chopped

3 spring onions (scallions), trimmed and thinly sliced

store-bought pickled green chillies (available from Asian supermarkets) to serve

---

Combine the stock, cinnamon stick, star anise, cloves, chillies, ginger and garlic in a large saucepan. Bring to a simmer over medium heat then reduce the heat to low, cover and simmer for 30 minutes to allow the flavours to infuse. Add the drained mushrooms, fish sauce, soy sauces and sugar, stirring until the sugar has dissolved. Cover and keep hot.

Bring a large saucepan of water to the boil. Add the choy sum and cook for 2–3 minutes or until wilted. Transfer to a colander to drain, reserving the boiling water.

Return the water to the pan, add the noodles and cook for 2–3 minutes over medium–high heat, or according to the packet instructions, until softened. Drain.

Divide the noodles among large bowls and place some choy sum on top of each. Place a piece of duck on top then pour over the stock and mushrooms. Scatter over the coriander, spring onion and pickled chillies and serve.

Beef and fermented tofu soup

· **SERVES 4** ·

We're not quite sure where or when we first had this, but the inspiration is Vietnamese and it's one of our all-time favourite soups. The crucial element here is fermented tofu, an ingredient of Chinese origin, which is also much-loved in Vietnam. It smells a bit funky, as any fermented food is wont to do, but it adds an incredible piquancy and burst of umami, and nothing else will really do in its place. It's cheap to buy and easy to find in Asian supermarkets, and comes in a few guises and flavours. However, you need the red variety here. Fermented tofu lasts for a long time in the refrigerator.

1½ tablespoons fish sauce

2 teaspoons caster (superfine) sugar

1½ tablespoons light soy sauce

2 eggs, well beaten

1 teaspoon freshly ground black pepper

500 g (1 lb 2 oz) beef fillet, trimmed and
    cut into 5 mm (¼ in) slices

SAUCE

3 pieces fermented red tofu,
    plus 2 teaspoons of the liquid

2½ tablespoons lime juice

1 tablespoon fish sauce

1 tablespoon light soy sauce

3 teaspoons caster (superfine) sugar

5 store-bought pickled garlic cloves (available from
    Asian supermarkets), finely chopped, plus extra to serve

4 red bird's eye chillies, thinly sliced

SOUP

150 g (5½ oz) dried cellophane (bean thread) noodles

1.5 litres (51 fl oz/6 cups) Beef stock (see page 14)

2½ tablespoons fish sauce

2 tablespoons soy sauce

500 g (1 lb 2 oz) thinly sliced Chinese cabbage (wombok)

large handful of coriander (cilantro) leaves,
    coarsely chopped

Combine the fish sauce, sugar, soy sauce and egg in a large bowl and whisk to mix well. Add the pepper and beef and stir to coat the beef. Cover the bowl with plastic wrap and refrigerate while you prepare the rest of the dish.

For the sauce, put the fermented tofu and tofu liquid in a bowl and, using a fork, mash well. Add the remaining ingredients and stir to mix well. Set aside.

For the soup, put the noodles in a large bowl, pour over enough cold water to cover then stand for 25 minutes or until softened. Drain well then, using kitchen scissors, cut into 5 cm (2 in) lengths.

Combine the stock, fish sauce and soy sauce in a large saucepan and bring to a simmer over medium heat. Add the noodles and cabbage and bring the liquid back to a simmer. Cook for 2–3 minutes or until the noodles are soft. Add the beef mixture, stirring constantly to separate the slices. Bring to a simmer then cook for 2–3 minutes or until the beef is tender. Stir in the coriander. Divide among large serving bowls and serve with the sauce for drizzling over and the extra pickled garlic on the side.

Chicken rice porridge

· SERVES 4–6 ·

Indonesians call this dish *bubur ayam,* which means chicken porridge or congee – a nod to its Chinese influence. You will find versions of this breakfast dish from street vendors to ritzy hotels. The dish comes alive with the addition of traditional condiments – spring onions (scallions), soy sauce and fried shallots, to name just a few.

200 g (7 oz/1 cup) jasmine rice, rinsed
1 fresh bay leaf
2 kaffir lime leaves
sea salt
ground white pepper

STOCK
2 chicken leg quarters
4 kaffir lime leaves, bruised
1 lemongrass stem, bruised and tied in a knot
2 cm (¾ in) piece fresh galangal, sliced
1 onion, halved and thickly sliced
4 garlic cloves, halved
3 cm (1¼ in) piece fresh turmeric, sliced,
    or ½ teaspoon ground turmeric

1 teaspoon ground coriander
1 teaspoon ground cumin
½ teaspoon freshly grated nutmeg

FRIED SOY BEANS
185 g (6½ oz/1 cup) dried soy beans, soaked
    in water overnight, drained
vegetable oil for shallow-frying

TO SERVE (OPTIONAL)
Chinese celery leaves
fried Chinese dough sticks (available from Asian
    supermarkets), sliced
rice crackers (available from Asian supermarkets)

For the stock, combine all the ingredients in a large saucepan with 1.5 litres (51 fl oz/6 cups) water. Bring to a simmer over medium heat, reduce the heat to low and cook for 25 minutes, or until the chicken is cooked through. Remove from the heat, transfer the chicken to a plate, strain the stock and reserve the liquid.

For the fried soy beans, put the beans in a saucepan over medium heat with enough water to cover. Bring to a simmer and cook over low heat for 45 minutes or until tender, adding extra water, if necessary, to keep the beans covered. Drain well then spread the beans in a single layer on a tray to cool. Remove any imperfect beans and loose shells/skin. Pat dry with paper towel.

Heat enough oil for shallow-frying in a large frying pan over medium heat (the oil should be about 1.5 cm/½ in deep). Add the beans, in batches if necessary, and cook for about 8 minutes or until golden and crisp. Drain well on paper towel.

Combine the rice, bay leaf and kaffir lime leaves in a medium saucepan and add 1.25 litres (42 fl oz/5 cups) of the reserved stock. Bring to a simmer and cook, stirring often, for 45 minutes or until the mixture is thick and the rice is starting to fall apart. Season to taste with sea salt and ground white pepper, thinning with some of the reserved stock if necessary. Reheat the remaining stock in a small saucepan and keep it hot.

Shred the chicken meat, discarding the fat and bones. Divide the rice mixture among large serving bowls, top with the shredded chicken and celery leaves, then pour some of the reserved stock into each bowl. Serve with the dough sticks, crackers and fried soy beans on the side.

Fish and pineapple sour soup

· SERVES 4–6 ·

Known as *canh chua ca,* which translates as 'sour fish soup', this dish originates from the Mekong Delta region of southern Vietnam and Cambodia. The soup requires the right Southeast Asian flavour notes – hot, sweet, sour and salty, which you can adjust to suit your own taste. Snapper, barramundi, blue eye cod or salmon would all work equally well here. For a vegetarian option you can use tofu and vegetable stock.

60 g (2 oz/¼ cup) tamarind pulp

250 ml (8½ fl oz/1 cup) boiling water

2 garlic cloves, crushed

1½ tablespoons vegetable oil

3 large lemongrass stems, white part only, thinly sliced

5 slices fresh galangal

45 g (1½ oz/¼ cup) shaved palm sugar (jaggery)

1.5 litres (51 fl oz/6 cups) fish stock or water

½ ripe, sweet pineapple (about 750 g/1 lb 11 oz) peeled, cored and cut into 1.5 cm (½ in) pieces

60 ml (2 fl oz/¼ cup) fish sauce

2 red bird's eye chillies, halved lengthways, plus extra to serve

3 ripe, firm tomatoes (about 250 g/9 oz in total), cut into wedges

4 Chinese celery stalks, cut into 2.5 cm (1 in) lengths, leaves reserved for garnish

200 g (7 oz) okra, trimmed and sliced lengthways

600 g (1 lb 5 oz) skin-on, firm white-fleshed fish, pin bones removed, cut into 2.5 cm (1 in) pieces

200 g (7 oz) mung bean sprouts

handful of rice paddy herb, coarsely sliced (optional)

handful of saw-tooth coriander (cilantro), coarsely sliced (optional)

ground white pepper

Thai basil to serve

lime cheeks to serve

Combine the tamarind pulp with the boiling water in a bowl and stand for 20 minutes. Strain the mixture through a sieve, using your fingers to press down on the solids to extract as much liquid as possible. Discard the solids.

In a large saucepan over medium heat, cook the garlic in the oil, stirring often, for 3 minutes or until it starts to turn golden. Add the lemongrass and continue cooking for 2 minutes. Add the galangal, sugar, stock and tamarind liquid and bring to a simmer. Reduce the heat to medium–low and cook, covered, for 5 minutes to allow the flavours to develop and the sugar to

dissolve. Add the pineapple, fish sauce, chilli, tomato, celery and okra and cook for 2–3 minutes or until the celery and okra start to soften. Add the fish and mung bean sprouts and cook for 3–4 minutes or until the fish is just cooked through. Stir in the herbs, if using, and season to taste with salt and ground white pepper.

Serve the soup in large bowls, garnish with Thai basil, with the lime cheeks and the extra sliced chillies on the side.

Tom kha gai

· SERVES 4–6 ·

Thai soups can be a meal in themselves, and this is a good example, especially with some steamed rice on the side. *Tom* translates as 'cooked' (in this case simmered in coconut milk), *kha* means galangal, and *gai* is chicken. Traditionally this soup uses bone-in chicken but, for ease, we have gone for boneless, skinless chicken thighs. You are most welcome to play around with the amounts, as there are no hard and fast rules here.

6 cm (2½ in) piece fresh ginger (preferably young ginger), cut into very fine matchsticks

2 lemongrass stems, bruised and tied in a knot

8 kaffir lime leaves

1.5 litres (51 fl oz/6 cups) Chicken stock (see page 14)

750 g (1 lb 11 oz) boneless, skinless chicken thighs, trimmed and thinly sliced

2½ tablespoons fish sauce

1 tablespoon shaved palm sugar (jaggery)

200 g (7 oz) fresh oyster mushrooms, large ones torn into pieces

150 g (5½ oz) tin bamboo shoots, drained and rinsed

400 ml (14 fl oz) coconut milk

60 ml (2 fl oz/¼ cup) lime juice

TO SERVE

coriander (cilantro) leaves

2 red bird's eye chillies, sliced

chilli oil

lime wedges

Combine the ginger and lemongrass in a large saucepan. Bruise half of the lime leaves and add them to the pan with the stock then bring to a simmer over medium–high heat. Reduce the heat to medium–low, cover and cook for 6–7 minutes to allow the flavours to develop.

Add the chicken, fish sauce, palm sugar, mushrooms and bamboo shoots, return to a simmer and cook for 2 minutes, or until the chicken is just cooked through. Add the coconut milk and continue to cook over low heat for 4–5 minutes or until heated through. Add the lime juice.

Remove the central vein from each of the remaining kaffir lime leaves, then cut the leaves into very fine shreds.

Divide the soup among large, warmed serving bowls and scatter over the shredded lime leaves, coriander and chilli. Drizzle with chilli oil and serve with the lime wedges on the side.

Seafood tom yum

· **SERVES 4** ·

Tom yum, which means 'sour soup', is hardly a novel dish. However, the ease with which it can be made, its great flexibility and, of course, that incomparable taste, make it a winner, so we felt the need to include it here. We've used an assortment of fresh seafood, but it's pretty standard to only use prawns – you can also use fish or chicken instead, or even pork (throw in thinly sliced pieces of trimmed fillet and cook for 2–3 minutes). You can adjust the hot, sour, salty and sweet notes to suit yourself but, strictly speaking, this soup should be spicy.

16 medium raw king prawns (shrimp)
2 litres (68 fl oz/8 cups) Chicken stock (see page 14)
  or fish stock
1 kg (2 lb 3 oz) mussels, scrubbed and debearded
80 g (2½ oz) Chilli jam (see page 21)
2 lemongrass stems, bruised
6 kaffir lime leaves, central vein removed, torn
12 slices fresh galangal

6 small green or red bird's eye chillies, halved lengthways
1 tablespoon caster (superfine) sugar
80 ml (2½ fl oz/⅓ cup) fish sauce
80 ml (2½ fl oz/⅓ cup) lime juice
12 scallops, roe on
200 g (7 oz) oyster mushrooms, torn
handful of coriander (cilantro) leaves, coarsely chopped

Peel the prawns, reserving the heads and shells. Cut the prawns in half lengthways, devein and refrigerate until needed.

Combine the shells and heads with the stock in a saucepan over medium heat, bring to a simmer then reduce the heat to low and cook for 40 minutes. Drop in the mussels and cook for 3 minutes or until they just open, then transfer the mussels to a bowl, using a slotted spoon.

Remove the mussel meat from half of the shells, leaving the remainder intact, and set aside. Strain the cooking liquid, discarding the solids, then return the stock to the pan with the chilli jam.

Cut the bruised lemongrass into 5 cm (2 in) lengths and add it to the stock with the lime leaves, galangal, chillies and sugar. Simmer for 5 minutes over medium heat then add the prawns, fish sauce, lime juice, scallops and mushrooms and stir well. Bring to a very gentle simmer and cook for 2–3 minutes or until the seafood is cooked through and the mushrooms are tender. Add the mussels and heat through. Season with salt and pepper to taste and add a little extra lime juice and fish sauce if necessary.

Divide among bowls, scatter over the coriander and serve.

Tamarind pork rib soup

· SERVES 4–6 ·

This rustic staple from the north of Thailand is about as basic a soup as you could make. What's more simple than pork bones (meaty ones though), the usual flavouring suspects and water all thrown into a pot and simmered away? The addition of tamarind imparts a great sour note. By all means substitute pieces of bone-in pork belly or pork hock, but you absolutely need bones for flavour. This soup is just as good, if not better, reheated and served the next day.

1.5 kg (3 lb 5 oz) pork spare ribs, cut into 5–7.5 cm (2–3 in) pieces (ask your butcher to do this)

1 teaspoon salt

1 tablespoon tamarind pulp

80 ml (2½ fl oz/⅓ cup) boiling water

60 ml (2 fl oz/¼ cup) yellow soy bean sauce

500 g (1 lb 2 oz) mustard greens, washed and cut into 5 cm (2 in) pieces

2 onions, each cut into 12 wedges

60 ml (2 fl oz/¼ cup) fish sauce

sea salt

Fried shallots (see page 26) to serve (optional)

PASTE

12 dried red chillies, soaked in boiling water for 30 minutes, drained, plus extra to garnish

2 lemongrass stems, white part only, roughly chopped

1 teaspoon salt

16 garlic cloves, halved

6 red Asian shallots, halved

1½ tablespoons gapi (Thai shrimp paste)

To make the paste, put the chillies, lemongrass, salt, garlic and shallots in a food processor and process to a rough paste. Alternatively, use a mortar and pestle. Mix in the gapi and set aside.

Put the pork ribs and salt in a large saucepan over medium heat with 2 litres (68 fl oz/8 cups) water or enough water to cover the ribs. Bring to the boil, skimming off any impurities that rise to the surface. Reduce the heat to low, add the paste and cook for 1–1½ hours or until the meat is very tender – it should pull away from the bone without any resistance.

Meanwhile, combine the tamarind pulp with the boiling water in a bowl and stand for 20 minutes. Strain the mixture through a sieve, using your fingers to press down on the solids to extract as much liquid as possible. Discard the solids.

Stir the tamarind liquid into the soup along with the yellow soy bean sauce, then add the mustard greens and onion. Simmer for 15–20 minutes or until the onion has softened and the greens are very tender. Stir in the fish sauce, season to taste with sea salt and freshly ground black pepper and serve scattered with the fried shallots, if using, and the extra dried red chillies.

Beef soto

· **SERVES 6** ·

This dish belongs to a whole family of soups found throughout Indonesia, called *soto*, and there are many variations. Based on a light, spiced broth, which in some versions is enriched with coconut milk, *soto* can be made using beef, tripe, tendons, pork, chicken and even water buffalo. This version is a meal in a bowl, complete with potato-based fritters and the unctuous shin meat.

2 tablespoons vegetable oil

2 lemongrass stems, bruised and tied in a knot

8 kaffir lime leaves, bruised

2 large onions, coarsely chopped

6 Chinese celery stalks

6 slices fresh galangal

1 cinnamon stick

2 star anise

½ nutmeg, cracked

1.5 kg (3 lb 5 oz) whole, boneless beef shins (about 3 shins), trimmed

100 ml (3½ fl oz) kecap manis

3 litres (101 fl oz/12 cups) Chicken stock (see page 14) or Beef stock (see page 14)

PASTE

3 cm (1¼ in) piece fresh ginger, chopped

6 large red Asian shallots, chopped

6 large garlic cloves, chopped

1 tablespoon ground coriander

BEEF AND POTATO FRITTERS

600 g (1 lb 5 oz) all-purpose potatoes (about 2 large), peeled and chopped

300 g (10½ oz) minced (ground) beef

2 eggs, beaten

1 teaspoon caster (superfine) sugar

4 spring onions (scallions), finely chopped

½ teaspoon freshly grated nutmeg

vegetable oil for shallow-frying

TO SERVE

250 g (9 oz) mung bean sprouts

2 large ripe tomatoes, cut into wedges

coriander (cilantro) leaves

Fried shallots (see page 26)

sambal oelek

For the paste, combine all the ingredients in a small food processor and process until a smooth paste forms. Alternatively, use a mortar and pestle.

In a large saucepan over medium heat, cook the paste in the oil, stirring, for 3–4 minutes. Add the lemongrass, kaffir lime leaves, onion, celery, galangal, cinnamon stick, star anise and nutmeg. Cook, stirring, for 2 minutes or until fragrant. Add the meat, kecap manis and enough stock to cover the shins. Slowly bring to a simmer, skimming any impurities that rise to the surface. Partially cover the pan and cook over low heat for 2½ hours or until the shin meat is very tender, adding a little extra water if necessary to keep the beef covered.

For the beef and potato fritters, cook the potatoes in boiling salted water until tender. Drain well then mash. Add the minced beef, egg, sugar, spring onion, nutmeg and season with salt and freshly ground black pepper to taste. Stir to combine well. Form the mixture into 24 flat discs about 5 cm (2 in) across.

In a large frying pan over medium heat, cook the fritters in the oil, in batches, until golden on both sides. Transfer to paper towel to drain any excess oil.

Remove the shins from the soup, then strain the stock, discarding the solids. Return the stock to the pan, skimming any impurities from the surface, then bring to a simmer. Thinly slice the beef.

Divide the meat between serving bowls, ladle over the stock and add a few fritters. Add the mung bean sprouts and tomato wedges and serve with the coriander and fried shallots scattered over, and the sambal oelek on the side.

Salads

Markets, markets, markets – whether we're in Laos, Thailand or on Java, we never tire of spending time in the food markets, ogling the variety of fruits, vegetables and herbs they sell, stacked in gleaming piles like edible jewels. The spanking freshness of everything, the buzz of commerce and the inevitable (and delicious) snacks on offer, never fail to excite us. When we're back home, where fruit and veg retail isn't quite as exciting, we boost ourselves by cooking from our repertoire of favourite Asian salads. Here are just a few of our most loved recipes.

Banana blossom salad

· SERVES 4–6 AS PART OF A SHARED MEAL ·

If you can get hold of banana blossoms, then you must try this incredible salad. Banana blossoms have a lovely, crisp texture and a neutral flavour not unlike artichoke hearts. You just use the creamy-coloured, tender inner leaves, but the pretty red outer leaves make nice serving vessels for the salad. Once cut, the interior of the 'leaves' discolour quickly, so the acidulated water step is necessary. This rich, creamy dressing also goes well with most crisp salads, or a salad using torn pieces of pomelo, prawns (shrimp), crushed roasted peanuts and finely sliced red Asian shallots.

juice of 1 lemon

1 tablespoon salt

2 banana blossoms

20 large cooked prawns (shrimp), shelled with tails left intact and deveined

3 spring onions (scallions), trimmed and finely shredded

30 g (1 oz/⅓ cup) fresh grated or thawed frozen grated coconut, lightly toasted (see page 28)

1 bunch of coriander (cilantro), coarsely chopped

40 g (1½ oz/¼ cup) toasted sesame seeds

DRESSING

1½ tablespoons small dried shrimp

2 tablespoons tamarind purée

1 tablespoon lime juice

2 tablespoons shaved palm sugar (jaggery)

2 tablespoons fish sauce

1 tablespoon Chilli jam (see page 21)

160 ml (5½ fl oz) coconut milk

For the dressing, coarsely grind the dried shrimp in an electric spice grinder. Combine with the remaining dressing ingredients in a bowl and stir until the sugar has dissolved.

Fill a large bowl with cold water then add the lemon juice and salt. Remove the red leaves from the banana blossoms and discard, reserving a few for serving the salad, if desired.

Working with one banana blossom at a time, remove the large, creamy 'leaves', taking out the small flower-like clusters between each one. Thinly slice the leaves diagonally. Immediately put the slices in the acidulated water to prevent them discolouring.

Cut the inner part of the banana blossom in half lengthways, then thinly slice diagonally, adding the slices to the acidulated water. Stand for 10 minutes then drain well and pat dry with paper towel.

Combine the drained, sliced leaves, prawns, spring onion and coconut in a large bowl and pour over the dressing. Add the coriander, toss to combine well, then divide the mixture among serving plates. Sprinkle over the sesame seeds and serve.

See image on pages 78–79.

Vegetable pickle salad

· SERVES 8 ·

Technically a sweet, sour and spicy pickle from Indonesia, Malaysia and Singapore, made from assorted vegetables and spices, we just love to eat *acar* as a salad. You are welcome to swap out the vegetables for varieties you prefer, or what's in season. Ours is based on a Nonya version from Penang. You'll find the pickle is better if left overnight, and you can easily halve the quantities to serve four. Serve it with Fried Nonya chicken (see page 168) and a side dish of Sticky rice (see page 28).

2 Lebanese (short) cucumbers, halved lengthways and seeded

1½ teaspoons salt

2 small carrots, peeled and cut into rounds

250 g (9 oz) snake (yard-long) beans, trimmed and cut into 3 cm (1¼ in) pieces

¼ cabbage, tough outer leaves removed, cored and cut into 3 cm (1¼ in) pieces

2 Japanese eggplants (aubergines), trimmed and cut into 1 cm (½ in) thick rounds

8 red Asian shallots, thinly sliced

6 garlic cloves, thinly sliced

2 tablespoons vegetable oil

100 ml (3½ fl oz) white vinegar

55 g (2 oz/¼ cup) caster (superfine) sugar

50 g (1¾ oz/⅓ cup) roasted unsalted peanuts, finely chopped

40 g (1½ oz/¼ cup) toasted sesame seeds to serve

PASTE

1 tablespoon belacan (Malaysian shrimp paste)

16 dried red chillies, soaked in boiling water for 30 minutes, drained

8 candlenuts, chopped

2 tablespoons chopped fresh turmeric or 2 teaspoons ground turmeric

2 tablespoons chopped fresh galangal

For the paste, wrap the belacan in foil. Heat a small, heavy-based frying pan over medium heat, add the wrapped belacan then dry-fry for 2 minutes on each side, or until fragrant. Cool and unwrap then transfer to a food processor with the remaining paste ingredients and process until a coarse paste forms. Alternatively, use a mortar and pestle. Set aside.

Cut the cucumbers into 2.5 cm (1 in) thick slices, put in a colander and sprinkle with the salt. Stand the colander over a sink for 20 minutes or until the cucumber has softened. Put the cucumber in a tea (dish) towel to dry any excess liquid.

Bring a saucepan of salted water to the boil. Add the carrot and cook for 1–2 minutes or until just starting to soften. Remove using a slotted spoon, transfer to a colander and drain well.

Repeat with the beans, cabbage and eggplant, draining each well. Transfer the drained vegetables to a clean tea towel to absorb any remaining liquid.

In a wok over medium heat, cook the paste, shallots and garlic in the oil, stirring constantly, for 2–3 minutes or until fragrant. Add the white vinegar, sugar and 80 ml (2½ fl oz/⅓ cup) water and bring to a simmer. Add the vegetables and toss to mix well. Cook, stirring gently to avoid breaking up the vegetables, for 3–4 minutes or until the vegetables are nearly cooked – they should still be a little crisp. Add the peanuts and cool to room temperature. Serve scattered with the sesame seeds. This salad will last about a week in the refrigerator.

Pork and eggplant salad

· SERVES 6 AS PART OF A SHARED MEAL ·

Here's a version of a favourite salad we first encountered years ago at Sompon Nabnian's famed Chiang Mai Thai Cooking School in north Thailand. In that region the flavours are fierce and somewhat herbal, and lack the tempering effects of coconut milk and sugar so prevalent in southern Thailand. If you've never eaten raw apple eggplant before, then do give this a go. It provides a fantastic, crisp, slightly bitter note to this rich yet rustic dish. Serve with a side of Sticky rice (see page 28).

1 tablespoon salt
500 g (1 lb 2 oz) apple eggplants (aubergines), thinly sliced
2 tablespoons vegetable oil
250 g (9 oz) minced (ground) pork, not too lean
2 tablespoons fish sauce
2 lemongrass stems, white part only, trimmed and thinly sliced
2 spring onions (scallions), trimmed and thinly sliced
2 large green chillies, thinly sliced

large handful of coriander (cilantro) sprigs
35 g (1¼ oz/½ cup) Fried shallots (see page 26)
lime wedges to serve

PASTE
10–12 green bird's eye chillies, coarsely chopped
8 small red Asian shallots, coarsely chopped
4 garlic cloves, coarsely chopped
1½ teaspoons gapi (Thai shrimp paste)

For the paste, combine all the ingredients in a small food processor and process until smooth. Alternatively, use a mortar and pestle.

Put the salt in a bowl filled with cold water, add the eggplant slices and stand for 10 minutes. Drain well and pat dry using paper towel.

Meanwhile, in a wok over medium–high heat, cook the paste in the oil, stirring, for 2–3 minutes or until the shallots in the paste lose their raw smell. Add the pork and cook, stirring to break up the meat, for 4–5 minutes or until the meat is cooked through. Stir in the fish sauce, add the drained eggplant slices and toss to combine well.

Remove the wok from the heat, add the lemongrass and three-quarters of the spring onion, chillies, coriander and fried shallots. Season well with freshly ground black pepper and toss to combine well.

Divide among serving bowls and scatter over the remaining spring onion, chilli, coriander and fried shallots. Serve warm or at room temperature with the lime wedges for squeezing over.

Chicken laab

· **SERVES 4** ·

It you asked lovers of Thai food to name their favourite salads, one would probably be green papaya salad, and another would be *laab*, also spelled *larb* or *laap* (meaning to mince/grind meat). This is a dish from the Isaan region of Thailand in the northeast of the country and bordered by Laos and Cambodia. It has many variations, from pork to duck, but we've opted for chicken. The most common complement to *laab* is Sticky rice (page 28). To serve, roll the rice in your hand into a ball and dip it into the *laab* to use as a scoop.

2½ tablespoons sticky (glutinous) rice

600 g (1 lb 5 oz) boneless, skinless chicken thighs, trimmed and roughly chopped

6 red Asian shallots, very thinly sliced

1 cm (½ in) piece fresh galangal, finely chopped

2 teaspoons caster (superfine) sugar

80 ml (2½ fl oz/⅓ cup) fish sauce

80 ml (2½ fl oz/⅓ cup) lime juice

1 tablespoon dried chilli flakes

1 lemongrass stem, white part only, very thinly sliced

5 kaffir lime leaves, central vein removed, very thinly sliced

2 spring onions (scallions), trimmed and thinly sliced

TO SERVE

small handful of mint leaves, coarsely chopped, plus extra whole leaves to garnish

small handful of coriander (cilantro) leaves

sliced fresh pineapple

1 tomato, quartered

sliced green chillies (optional)

Heat a small heavy-based frying pan over medium heat. Add the rice and toast, shaking the pan often, for 6–8 minutes or until golden. Cool, then transfer to an electric spice grinder and grind to a coarse powder. Alternatively, use a mortar and pestle. Set aside.

Using a large, sharp knife, chop the chicken until it is coarsely minced (ground). Alternatively, cut the chicken into small pieces then process it in a food processor using the pulse button, taking care not to over-process – the chicken mince should still have some texture.

Put the chicken in a bowl with the shallots, galangal, sugar, fish sauce, lime juice, chilli flakes and lemongrass and toss to coat well. Cover the bowl with plastic wrap and stand for 30 minutes.

Heat a wok over medium heat, add the chicken mixture and cook, stirring constantly to break up the meat, for about 8 minutes or until the chicken is cooked through but not coloured. Transfer, with any juices, to a bowl. Add the remaining ingredients to the bowl, including the rice powder, and toss to combine well. Cool slightly. Transfer to a serving bowl, scatter over the mint and coriander leaves and serve warm or at room temperature with the pineapple slices, tomato and green chillies, if using.

Green vegetable salad with coconut

· SERVES 4–6 AS PART OF A SHARED MEAL ·

We think Javanese food is really underrated. It tends to be more rustic than other Asian cuisines and maybe not as 'pretty', but it's full of punchy flavours. This salad, known as *urap* in Bahasa, can be re-jigged according to whatever (usually green) vegetables are in season. Try blanched taro leaves, green beans or thinly sliced cucumbers. What isn't negotiable, though, is the use of fresh grated coconut in the dressing – don't even think of using desiccated. Luckily the thawed frozen stuff comes to the rescue of the time-strapped, so make sure you stock up on some.

300 g (10½ oz) cabbage leaves

450 g (1 lb) silverbeet (Swiss chard) leaves (about 1 bunch), white ribs removed

250 g (9 oz) snake (yard-long) beans, trimmed and cut into 1 cm (½ in) pieces

250 g (9 oz) bean sprouts

2 large kaffir lime leaves, central vein removed, very thinly sliced

2 large green chillies, trimmed and cut into very fine matchsticks

50 g (1¾ oz/¾ cup) Fried shallots (see page 26), plus extra for serving

100 g (3½ oz/1 cup) fresh grated or thawed frozen grated coconut, toasted (see page 28)

DRESSING

4 garlic cloves, chopped

6 green bird's eye chillies, chopped

3 teaspoons fresh turmeric, chopped, or ¾ teaspoon ground turmeric

6 large kaffir lime leaves, central vein removed, chopped

60 g (2 oz/⅓ cup) shaved palm sugar (jaggery)

80 ml (2½ fl oz/⅓ cup) lime juice

For the dressing, combine the garlic, chillies, turmeric and lime leaves in a small food processor and process until a smooth paste forms. Add the palm sugar and lime juice and process until smooth and the sugar has dissolved.

Meanwhile, bring a saucepan fitted with a large steamer and half-filled with salted water to the boil over high heat. Add the cabbage leaves and cook, covered, for 2–3 minutes or until softened. Using tongs, transfer to a colander and leave to drain.

Put the silverbeet in the steamer and cook for 1–2 minutes or until wilted then transfer to the colander. Cook the snake beans in the same way for 2–3 minutes, and the bean sprouts for 1 minute, then cool the vegetables to room temperature.

Thinly slice the cabbage and silverbeet and combine in a large bowl with the other steamed vegetables, the sliced lime leaves, chillies, fried shallots and 70 g (2½ oz/⅔ cup) of the coconut. Add the dressing, season well with salt and freshly ground black pepper then toss to coat. Serve immediately with the remaining coconut and the extra fried shallots scattered on top.

Grilled beef and mushroom salad

· SERVES 4 AS PART OF A SHARED MEAL ·

This dish is an amalgamation of a few salads we love from Thailand. *Yam neua*, or grilled beef salad, is a Thai classic. However, this dish takes a northern turn and we think of it as a kind of mushroom laab with grilled steak thrown in for good measure (feel free to leave this out for a more vegetarian-friendly version if you prefer). What it lacks in total authenticity, it makes up for in deliciousness – mushrooms and red meat are a natural pairing. We'd even go so far as to suggest grilled, sliced lamb backstraps instead of the beef, even though lamb isn't exactly the most Thai of meats.

1½ tablespoons sticky (glutinous) rice

2 x 200 g (7 oz) beef Scotch fillet steaks, excess fat trimmed

vegetable oil for brushing

sea salt

450 g (1 lb) oyster mushrooms, large ones halved

1 red onion, halved and very thinly sliced

1 bunch of mint, leaves torn

1 bunch of coriander (cilantro), leaves torn

lime cheeks to serve

DRESSING

3 teaspoons dried chilli flakes

1 lemongrass stem, white part only, very thinly sliced

3 teaspoons caster (superfine) sugar

80 ml (2½ fl oz/⅓ cup) fish sauce

2 tablespoons light soy sauce

80 ml (2½ fl oz/⅓ cup) lime juice

60 ml (2 fl oz/¼ cup) Beef stock (see page 14), warm

1 tablespoon freshly ground black pepper

Heat a small, heavy-based frying pan over medium heat, add the rice then toast, shaking the pan often, for about 8 minutes or until golden. Cool, then transfer to an electric spice grinder and grind to a coarse powder. Alternatively, use a mortar and pestle. Set aside.

Heat a chargrill pan or barbecue to high. Brush the steak with oil, season well with sea salt and freshly ground black pepper and cook for 4 minutes on each side, depending on thickness, or until medium–rare. Transfer the meat to a plate and rest for 10–15 minutes.

Drizzle the mushrooms with oil then grill, in batches, for 6 minutes, turning once, or until softened and lightly charred.

Meanwhile, for the dressing, combine all the ingredients in a large bowl and stir until the sugar has dissolved.

Thinly slice the steak, reserving any juices that have collected.

Add the mushrooms and meat to the dressing in the bowl with the onion, any reserved juices, the mint and coriander. Toss to combine well then serve immediately with the lime cheeks.

Fried egg salad

· SERVES 4 ·

The Thais call this simple salad *yam khai dao* and, on every level it's our kind of dish. It's easy to rustle up when the pantry is looking empty and is great for brunch, lunch or dinner. The key is to fry the eggs until they are crisp and golden, but it's totally up to you if you want your yolks runny, firm or somewhere in between. Try using quail eggs for a daintier dish.

2½ tablespoons dried shrimp, soaked in warm water for 30 minutes, drained and coarsely chopped

125 ml (4 fl oz/½ cup) vegetable oil

8 eggs

1 butter lettuce, leaves washed, dried and torn

1 red onion, cut into thin wedges

1 carrot, peeled and shredded into fine ribbons or cut into matchsticks

handful of coriander (cilantro) leaves

handful of Thai basil leaves

2 red bird's eye chillies, thinly sliced

DRESSING

80 ml (2½ fl oz/⅓ cup) lime juice

1½ tablespoons fish sauce

1 tablespoon shaved palm sugar (jaggery)

2 garlic cloves, crushed

3 red bird's eye chillies, thinly sliced

In a wok over medium heat, fry the dried shrimp in the oil for about 2 minutes or until crisp and fragrant. Using a slotted spoon, transfer to a plate lined with paper towel to drain any excess oil. Reserve the hot oil in the wok.

Increase the heat to medium–high and, working in batches, add 4 eggs to the hot oil in the wok, taking care as the oil will splutter. Cook for 1 minute or until the egg whites are puffy and golden on the bottom. Carefully turn the eggs over using a spatula, then cook for another 20–30 seconds or until the tops are just set, but the yolks are still runny. Transfer to a plate lined with paper towel to drain any excess oil. Repeat with the remaining eggs.

For the dressing, combine all the ingredients in a bowl and stir to combine well and until the sugar has dissolved.

Divide the eggs between four bowls. Add the dressing, fried dried shrimp, lettuce, onion, carrot, herbs and chillies and toss to combine well. Serve immediately.

Chicken and cabbage salad

· **SERVES 4** ·

Often referred to as 'Vietnamese coleslaw', this salad, called *goi bap cai ga*, is positively addictive and incredibly easy to make. Chicken, pork, prawns (shrimp) or a combination of these are commonly added to the cabbage base – just take care not to overcook the chicken; it should have a wonderful (almost) slippery texture, which comes from very gentle, slow simmering. Serve this as a light summer main course accompanied by plenty of steamed rice. Note that Asian supermarkets sell grooved, hand-held peelers that take the work out of achieving long, thin, elegantly shredded vegetables.

1 x 1.25 kg (2 lb 12 oz) chicken

1 lemongrass stem, bruised and tied in a knot

4 kaffir lime leaves

6 slices of fresh ginger

Vietnamese pickled onion (see page 27)

350 g (12½ oz) cabbage, hard core removed,
    very thinly sliced

2 Lebanese (short) cucumbers, cut into fine matchsticks

1 large carrot, peeled and shredded into fine ribbons
    or cut into matchsticks

handful of Vietnamese mint leaves

handful of mint leaves

handful of perilla leaves, large ones torn

80 g (2¾ oz/½ cup) roasted unsalted peanuts,
    crushed, plus extra to serve

DRESSING

55 g (2 oz/¼ cup) caster (superfine) sugar

125 ml (4 fl oz/½ cup) rice vinegar

125 ml (4 fl oz/½ cup) lime juice

125 ml (4 fl oz/½ cup) fish sauce

3 medium red chillies, thinly sliced

TO SERVE

35 g (1¼ oz/½ cup) Fried shallots (see page 26)

prawn crackers

Put the chicken in a saucepan large enough to hold it snugly. Add the lemongrass, lime leaves and ginger and enough cold water to just cover the chicken. Slowly bring to a very gentle simmer over medium–low heat – bubbles should only just be breaking the surface. Cover and cook the chicken for 45 minutes, taking care not to let the water simmer too vigorously.

Remove the pan from the heat and stand, covered, until the liquid is cool. Remove the chicken and reserve the liquid for another use. Using your fingers, coarsely shred the chicken, discarding the skin and bones.

Combine the chicken, pickled onion, cabbage, cucumber and carrot in a bowl and toss to combine. Add the herbs and peanuts and toss again.

For the dressing, stir the sugar, rice vinegar and lime juice in a bowl until the sugar has dissolved. Add the fish sauce and chillies then pour over the salad. Toss well then divide among plates. Scatter over some extra crushed peanuts and fried shallots and serve with the prawn crackers.

Vegetable salad with peanut sauce

· **SERVES 4–6** ·

This salad, known locally as *pecel*, is a signature dish of the central Javanese town of Solo and is as delicious as it sounds. It's a substantial mix of assorted, steamed leafy vegetables served with a luxuriant cooked peanut sauce and finished with all manner of crisp, crunchy fried things, such as tempeh and prawn crackers.

1 large bunch of water spinach (morning glory), trimmed and washed

8 wing beans, trimmed and thinly sliced diagonally

300 g (10½ oz) mung bean sprouts

2 bunches of English spinach, trimmed and washed

1 bunch of snake (yard-long) beans, trimmed and cut into 1 cm (½ in) pieces

500 ml (17 fl oz/2 cups) vegetable oil

200 g (7 oz) tempeh, thinly sliced

prawn crackers to serve

1 telegraph (long) cucumber, peeled and thinly sliced

125 g (4½ oz) fried tofu puffs (available from Asian supermarkets), sliced, to serve

PEANUT SAUCE

3 teaspoons tamarind pulp

60 ml (2 fl oz/¼ cup) boiling water

2 teaspoons trasi (Indonesian shrimp paste)

300 g (10½ oz) raw peanuts

300 ml (10 fl oz) vegetable oil

5 cm (2 in) piece fresh galangal, chopped

8 red bird's eye chillies, chopped

5 garlic cloves, chopped

80 g (2¾ oz) shaved palm sugar (jaggery)

10 kaffir lime leaves, central vein removed, chopped

For the peanut sauce, combine the tamarind pulp with the boiling water in a bowl and stand for 20 minutes. Strain the mixture through a sieve, using your fingers to press down on the solids to extract as much liquid as possible. Discard the solids.

Wrap the trasi in foil. Heat a small, heavy-based frying pan over medium heat, add the wrapped trasi then dry-fry for 2 minutes on each side, or until fragrant. Cool and unwrap.

In a wok over medium heat, cook the peanuts in the oil for 4 minutes or until golden. Using a slotted spoon, transfer to paper towel. Cool.

Combine the peanuts, trasi, galangal, chillies, garlic, palm sugar and kaffir lime leaves in a food processor and process until smooth. Add the tamarind liquid and 340 ml (11½ fl oz/1⅓ cups) water and process until creamy.

Bring a large saucepan of water to the boil. Add the water spinach and cook for 1–2 minutes or until just tender. Transfer to a bowl of iced water, drain well then transfer to a clean tea (dish) towel. Repeat with the wing beans, mung bean sprouts, spinach and snake beans.

Heat the oil in a saucepan to 170°C (340°F), or until a cube of bread turns golden in 20 seconds. Add the tempeh and cook for 4–5 minutes or until golden. Using a slotted spoon, transfer to paper towel and drain well. In batches, as they will quickly expand, add the prawn crackers to the oil in the pan and cook for 1 minute or until puffed and crisp, then transfer to paper towel to drain. Arrange the cooked vegetables, tempeh, sliced cucumber and tofu puffs on a large serving dish. Spoon over the peanut sauce and serve with the prawn crackers on the side.

Raw fish salad

· **SERVES 4–6 AS PART OF A SHARED MEAL** ·

Versions of *laab* (the word comes from a northern Thai term meaning 'to mince/grind meat') are common throughout northeastern Thailand and Laos. There are many different types. The use of raw flesh – either pork, buffalo, beef or fish is not uncommon. This raw fish salad is our general ode to those rugged, herb and chilli–laced *laab*, with their bracing jolt of lime juice, although we have steered a little off-course by slicing instead of chopping the fish. Serve with Sticky rice (see page 28).

1 tablespoon prahok (fermented fish paste)
6 large dried red chillies
50 g (2 oz/¼ cup) sticky (glutinous) rice
750 g (1 lb 11 oz) skinless snapper or other firm white-fleshed fish fillets
½ teaspoon salt
60 ml (2 fl oz/¼ cup) lime juice
4 red Asian shallots, very thinly sliced

2 lemongrass stems, white part only, very thinly sliced
handful of mint leaves, very thinly sliced, some whole leaves reserved to garnish
handful of coriander (cilantro) leaves
handful of saw-tooth coriander (cilantro) leaves (optional)
4 spring onions (scallions), trimmed and thinly sliced
4–5 green bird's eye chillies, sliced, to serve

Combine the prahok in a small saucepan with 60 ml (2 fl oz/¼ cup) water and bring to a simmer over medium heat. Cook for 2 minutes then remove from the heat and cool. Strain well, pressing down on the solids in the sieve with the back of a spoon to extract as much liquid as possible. Set aside. Discard the solids.

Heat a small, heavy-based frying pan over medium heat. Add the dried chillies and dry-fry for 6–7 minutes, turning occasionally, or until dark red and crisp. Remove from the heat and cool.

Use your fingers to crumble the chillies coarsely. Set aside.

Reheat the frying pan to medium–high, add the rice and toast, shaking the pan occasionally, for 6–8 minutes or until golden. Transfer to an electric spice grinder and grind to a coarse powder. Alternatively, use a mortar and pestle. Set aside with the chillies.

Thinly slice the fish. Combine in a bowl with the salt and lime juice and toss to combine well. Stand for 20 minutes. Add the prahok liquid, chillies, rice powder, shallots, lemongrass, herbs and spring onion and toss to combine well.

Transfer to a serving platter, scatter over some whole mint leaves and the green chillies and serve.

Lime-marinated beef salad

· SERVES 4–6 AS PART OF A SHARED MEAL ·

While inspired by Cambodian versions of this dish (called *plear sach ko* in Khmer), 'cooking' raw meat in citrus juices is also a popular technique in Vietnam. The strong acids in the lime tenderise the meat, while herbs and chilli add freshness. Prahok is synonymous with Khmer food and it imparts an important background flavour. The secret to achieving thin, even meat slices is to tightly roll the beef in plastic wrap, place it in the freezer and slice it while it's still semi-frozen.

500 g (1 lb 2 oz) piece of beef fillet, trimmed
190 ml (6½ fl oz/¾ cup) lime juice
45 g (1½ oz/¼ cup) shaved palm sugar (jaggery)
3 garlic cloves, crushed
1 lemongrass stem, white part only, finely chopped
1 teaspoon freshly ground black pepper
1 tablespoon prahok (fermented fish paste)
60 ml (2 fl oz/¼ cup) boiling water

60 ml (2 fl oz/¼ cup) fish sauce
1 large red onion, cut into thin rings
large handful of Thai basil leaves
large handful of mint leaves
2 tablespoons roasted unsalted peanuts, lightly crushed
2 tablespoons toasted sesame seeds
200 g (7 oz) mung bean sprouts

SALADS

Wrap the beef tightly in plastic wrap so it has a neat shape, then place it in the freezer for 40–50 minutes or until partially frozen – do not let it freeze. Using a sharp knife, cut the beef into 2–3 mm (¹⁄₁₆–⅛ in) thick slices, then place the slices in a bowl.

Combine half the lime juice, 1 tablespoon of the palm sugar, half the garlic, the lemongrass and pepper in a bowl and stir to combine well. Add to the beef, stirring to coat. Cover the bowl with plastic wrap and stand at room temperature for 30 minutes.

Drain the beef well, squeezing gently with your hands to remove as much of the liquid as possible. Discard the liquid.

Combine the prahok in a small saucepan with 60 ml (2 fl oz/¼ cup) water and bring to a simmer over medium heat. Cook for 2 minutes then remove from the heat and cool. Strain well, pressing down on the solids in the sieve with the back of a spoon to extract as much liquid as possible. Set aside. Discard the solids.

Combine the prahok liquid with the remaining lime juice, remaining sugar and remaining garlic with the fish sauce in a bowl and stir well.

In a large bowl combine the beef, half the onion, half the herbs, the peanuts, sesame seeds and mung bean sprouts. Add the dressing and toss to combine. Divide among plates, scatter over the remaining onion and herbs and serve.

Squid and wing bean salad

· SERVES 4 ·

A couple of hours south of Bangkok, the old town of Phetchaburi is famous for several things – palm fruit curry, extraordinary desserts and Khao Wang, a famous old royal palace complex. After taking in the sights, we like nothing more than relaxing in the atmospheric riverside dining room at Rabieng Rimnum guesthouse, eating dishes like this refreshing salad.

600 g (1 lb 5 oz) fresh squid, cleaned, tentacles reserved
400 g (14 oz) wing beans, trimmed and sliced about 1 cm (½ in) thick
90 g (3 oz) watercress sprigs
1 small red onion, halved and thinly sliced
4 hard-boiled eggs, quartered
3–4 red bird's eye chillies, thinly sliced
handful of coriander (cilantro) leaves
handful of mint leaves
2½ tablespoons toasted sesame seeds

DRESSING
3 garlic cloves, chopped
grated zest of 1 lime
2½ tablespoons shaved palm sugar (jaggery)
80 ml (2½ fl oz/⅓ cup) lime juice
1½ tablespoons fish sauce
60 ml (2 fl oz/¼ cup) Sweet chilli sauce (see page 15)
160 ml (5½ fl oz) coconut milk

Cut the squid tubes into 1.5 cm (½ in) thick pieces and set aside with the tentacles.

For the dressing, combine all the ingredients in a food processor and process until smooth.

Bring a large saucepan of salted water to the boil over medium–high heat. Add the squid and cook for 1–2 minutes, or until tender and just cooked through. Drain well.

Combine the wing beans in a large bowl with the squid, watercress, red onion, eggs, chillies and herbs and gently toss to combine. Drizzle over the dressing then place on a serving platter. Scatter over the sesame seeds and serve.

Curries

Can there be another dish with a more fragrant allure than curry? Heady with spices, redolent with the freshest of herbs and spiked with the hot jolt of chilli, the curries of Southeast Asia are like no other and are wildly varied. Some are made with the soothing creaminess of coconut milk, while others have sour or bitter notes and are not as rich. Yet others are dry, spiced-up sautés. Maybe the most familiar curries are those drenched in opulent, flavoursome gravy. Whatever the style or the main ingredient, cooking a curry from scratch is nothing short of an adventure.

Fish and eggplant green curry

· **SERVES 4** ·

Green curry comes from the Central Plains region of Thailand and gets its colour from the liberal use of fresh green chillies in the foundation paste. Like all spice pastes, this tastes fresher, somehow, if you make it by hand, pounding everything together using a mortar and pestle – the pounding action breaks down the paste components smoothly, melding them together into an unctuous pulp. Food processors and blenders are a little brutal, as their cutting action shatters the fibres and results in a coarser paste. However, it's way easier to make a paste in a processor (and far better than using a purchased one). Adding a little water as you go can make the process a bit easier.

1 quantity Green curry paste (see page 22)

2 tablespoons vegetable oil

250 ml (8½ fl oz/1 cup) Chicken stock (see page 14)

400 ml (14 fl oz) coconut milk

45 g (1½ oz/¼ cup) shaved palm sugar (jaggery)

700 g (1 lb 9 oz) blue eye cod, barramundi, snapper or other firm white-fleshed fish fillets, skin left on and cut into 5 cm (2 in) pieces

2 tablespoons fish sauce

4 kaffir lime leaves, bruised

110 g (4 oz/¾ cup) pea eggplants (aubergines)

large handful of Thai basil leaves to serve

Fried shallots (see page 26) to serve

In a large saucepan over medium heat, cook the curry paste in the oil, stirring, for 2–3 minutes or until fragrant. Add the stock, coconut milk and palm sugar and bring to a simmer. Add the fish and bring the mixture back to a gentle simmer. Cook for 2 minutes or until the fish is half cooked. Add the fish sauce, kaffir lime leaves and eggplant and cook for 2 minutes more or until the fish is cooked through – the eggplant should still be crunchy. Season to taste with a little more fish sauce if desired, then serve with the basil leaves and fried shallots scattered over.

See image on pages 106–107.

Curried eggs with roti jala

· SERVES 4–6 AS PART OF A SHARED MEAL ·

Don't let the name put you off – we're not talking the old-fashioned filling for sandwiches here! This is an Indonesian dish, which you can have as a main meal with some simple steamed rice, or as an accompaniment to a more complex meal. Coconut and eggs work well together and, with the addition of fried shallots, you get smooth, creamy and crunchy textures all in one dish.

1 tablespoon tamarind pulp
80 ml (2½ fl oz/⅓ cup) boiling water
2 tablespoons vegetable oil
500 ml (17 fl oz/2 cups) coconut milk
1 lemongrass stem, bruised and tied in a knot
8 hard-boiled eggs

ROTI JALA
275 g (9½ oz) plain (all-purpose) flour
2 eggs
300 ml (10 fl oz) coconut milk
1 teaspoon salt
vegetable oil for frying

PASTE
8 small red Asian shallots, chopped
4 garlic cloves, chopped
6 red bird's eye chillies, chopped
3 cm (1¼ in) piece fresh ginger, coarsely chopped
2.5 cm (1 in) piece fresh galangal, coarsely chopped
2½ teaspoons chopped fresh turmeric or ½ teaspoon ground turmeric

TO SERVE
sliced spring onions (scallions)
Fried shallots (see page 26)

Combine the tamarind pulp with the boiling water in a bowl and stand for 20 minutes. Strain the mixture through a sieve, using your fingers to press down on the solids to extract as much liquid as possible. Discard the solids.

For the roti jala, put the flour, eggs, coconut milk, salt and 250 ml (8½ fl oz/1 cup) water in a food processor and process until smooth. Add a little extra water if necessary to form a smooth, creamy battter.

Lightly oil a heavy-based frying pan over medium heat. Dip the fingers of one hand into the batter then swirl the batter from your fingers, dripping it over the base of the pan to form a lacy pancake. Cook for 1–2 minutes or until set, then turn over and cook for a further minute or so.

For the paste, combine all the ingredients in a food processor and process until a smooth paste forms. Alternatively, use a mortar and pestle.

In a saucepan or wok over medium heat, cook the paste in the oil, stirring, for 2–3 minutes, or until fragrant. Add the coconut milk, lemongrass and tamarind liquid and bring to a simmer. Reduce the heat to low and cook, covered, for 10 minutes to allow the flavours to develop. Add the eggs then simmer, uncovered, for 6–7 minutes or until the liquid has reduced slightly. Serve garnished with the spring onions and fried shallots, with the roti jala, folded into quarters if desired.

Yellow curry with mussels

· SERVES 4 ·

It's fair to say that Cambodian, or Khmer, food, is a lesser known Southeast Asian cuisine. If you haven't been to Cambodia, then take our word for it when we say the food is really, really extraordinary. They tend to be less liberal with chilli and sugar, but unique in their love for prahok, a pungent fermented fish paste. Warning – this product has a whiff to it like no other, but don't let that put you off. What it does to food is magical, and it adds a pronounced saltiness and tang to this dish. In Laos they call their version padek, and even use it as a dip for vegetables.

2 tablespoons prahok (fermented fish paste)

1 large red capsicum (bell pepper), trimmed, seeded and cut into thin strips

1 quantity Yellow curry paste (see page 22)

2 tablespoons vegetable oil

2 kg (4 lb 6 oz) small black mussels, scrubbed and debearded

60 ml (2 fl oz/¼ cup) fish sauce

2½ tablespoons shaved palm sugar (jaggery)

500 ml (17 fl oz/2 cups) coconut milk

8 kaffir lime leaves, central vein removed, very thinly sliced

TO SERVE

large handful of Thai basil leaves

lime halves

Combine the prahok with 125 ml (4 fl oz/½ cup) water in a small saucepan over medium heat. Bring to a simmer and cook for 2–3 minutes. Strain well, pressing on the solids in the sieve with the back of a spoon to extract as much liquid as possible. Discard the solids and set the liquid aside.

In a large wok over medium–high heat, cook the capsicum and curry paste in the oil, stirring constantly, for 2–3 minutes or until fragrant. Add the mussels and toss to combine well. Add the fish sauce, palm sugar, coconut milk, prahok liquid and kaffir lime leaves, cover the wok and cook, shaking the wok occasionally, for 3 minutes or just until the mussels open. Scatter over the basil leaves and serve immediately with the lime halves served separately for squeezing.

Beef brisket curry

· SERVES 6 ·

Oh, brisket, how we do love you! And here's an interesting factoid about this deeply flavoursome cut of meat – cows don't have collar bones so their pectoral muscles (the brisket) have to support 60 per cent of their standing weight. Hence this cut is full of connective tissue and requires long, slow cooking in order to become tender. This is a different sort of a curry. It's rustic and Thai in inspiration, with a relatively simple foundation paste and no coconut cream. What makes it really interesting are the assorted bits and pieces you scatter over at the end.

1.2 kg (2 lb 10 oz) beef brisket, cut into
   1 cm (½ in) thick slices
2 tablespoons vegetable oil
2½ tablespoons shaved palm sugar (jaggery)
60 ml (2 fl oz/¼ cup) fish sauce

CURRY PASTE

2½ teaspoons belacan (Malaysian shrimp paste)
3 teaspoons coriander seeds
1½ teaspoons cumin seeds
12 dried red chillies, soaked in boiling water for
   30 minutes, drained
6 garlic cloves, chopped
5 cm (2 in) piece fresh ginger, chopped
2 lemongrass stems, white part only, chopped

6 red Asian shallots, chopped
1 tablespoon chopped fresh or 1 teaspoon
   ground turmeric

TO SERVE

300 g (10½ oz) firm tofu, cut into 1 cm (½ in) cubes
6 hard-boiled eggs, halved
145 g (5 oz/1 cup) salted radish (available from Asian
   supermarkets), rinsed
120 g (4½ oz/¾ cup) roasted unsalted peanuts, lightly
   crushed
3 spring onions (scallions), trimmed and thinly sliced
   diagonally
coriander (cilantro) sprigs

For the curry paste, wrap the belacan in foil. Heat a small, heavy-based frying pan over medium heat, add the wrapped belacan then dry-fry for 2 minutes on each side, or until fragrant. Cool and unwrap.

In the same frying pan over medium heat, dry-fry the coriander and cumin seeds, shaking the pan occasionally, for 2–3 minutes or until fragrant. Cool slightly, then transfer to an electric spice grinder and grind to a coarse powder. Alternatively, use a mortar and pestle.

Combine the drained dried chillies, belacan, coriander and cumin mixture and all the remaining paste ingredients in a food processor and process until a coarse paste forms, adding a little water if necessary. Alternatively, use a mortar and pestle.

Bring a large saucepan of water to the boil, add the beef, in 2 batches, and cook for 1 minute or until the meat changes colour. Drain well and set aside.

In a large saucepan over medium heat, cook the curry paste in the oil, stirring, for 3 minutes or until fragrant. Add the beef and 875 ml (29½ fl oz/3½ cups) water and bring to a simmer. Reduce the heat to low and cook for 1 hour 45 minutes or until the beef is very tender. Stir in the palm sugar and fish sauce and cook for 2–3 minutes or until the sugar has dissolved. Serve with the tofu, eggs, salted radish, peanuts, spring onion and coriander passed separately to scatter over.

Lamb shank curry

· **SERVES 4–6** ·

As Indonesia is a predominantly Muslim country, beef and goat are widely eaten. Lamb fits the halal profile too and, although not as common, is also consumed. Lamb shanks, with their fall-apart tenderness and sweet meaty savour, work perfectly with assertive curry flavours, even though lamb cooked in large pieces like this is not strictly traditional. Indonesian curries can be complex, using both plenty of dry spices (cardamom, nutmeg, coriander, cloves and the like) as well as 'wet' aromatics like lemongrass, fresh chillies, galangal and kaffir lime leaves.

8 frenched lamb shanks

2½ tablespoons vegetable oil

2½ tablespoons white vinegar

8 cardamom pods, bruised

6 whole cloves

large pinch of freshly grated nutmeg

2 lemongrass stems, bruised and tied in a knot

500 ml (17 fl oz/2 cups) coconut milk

PASTE

1½ tablespoons coriander seeds

1 teaspoon trasi (Indonesian shrimp paste)

8 large red Asian shallots, chopped

6 garlic cloves, chopped

8 large red chillies, chopped

1½ tablespoons chopped fresh ginger

1½ tablespoons chopped fresh galangal

1 tablespoon chopped fresh turmeric or
   1½ teaspoons ground turmeric

6 candlenuts, chopped

TO SERVE

thinly sliced red bird's eye chillies

Thai basil leaves

Chilli sambal (see page 18)

CURRIES

For the paste, heat a small, heavy-based frying pan over medium–low heat, add the coriander seeds and dry-fry, shaking the pan, for 3 minutes or until fragrant. Transfer to an electric spice grinder and grind to a coarse powder. Alternatively, use a mortar and pestle.

Wrap the trasi in foil. Heat a small, heavy-based frying pan over medium heat, add the wrapped trasi then dry-fry for 2 minutes on each side, or until fragrant. Cool and unwrap. Transfer to a food processor with the ground coriander seeds and remaining paste ingredients and process until a smooth paste forms, adding a little water if necessary.

In a wok or frying pan over medium–high heat, cook the lamb shanks in the oil, in batches, turning often, for 5 minutes or until browned all over. Transfer to a bowl.

Remove all but 2 tablespoons of the oil from the wok, add the paste and cook, stirring often, for 3 minutes or until fragrant. Return the meat to the wok and add the remaining ingredients, except the coconut milk. Add 1.5 litres (51 fl oz/6 cups) water or enough to just cover the shanks. Bring to a simmer, reduce the heat to low and cook for 1½ hours or until the meat is tender. Add the coconut milk, bring back to a simmer and cook for 10 minutes or until the meat is very tender.

Serve garnished with the sliced chilli and basil leaves, with the chilli sambal passed separately.

Northern Thai pork curry

· **SERVES 4–6** ·

Called *gaeng hanglay* in northern Thailand, this curry can be made with pork or beef, so it's not too dissimilar to the classic massaman curry. For this recipe we've opted for pork neck, but pork belly or shoulder work equally well. The taste improves if left overnight, so cook a double batch and freeze for future use.

2 tablespoons tamarind pulp

190 ml (6½ fl oz/¾ cup) boiling water

1.5 kg (3 lb 5 oz) pork neck, cut into 1.5 cm (½ in) slices

2–3 tablespoons vegetable oil

12 small red Asian shallots, sliced

8 cm (3¼ in) piece fresh ginger, cut into fine matchsticks

60 ml (2 fl oz/¼ cup) fish sauce

60 ml (2 fl oz/¼ cup) light soy sauce

4 pickled garlic bulbs (available from Asian supermarkets), cloves separated

2½ tablespoons shaved palm sugar (jaggery)

100 g (3½ oz) blanched roasted peanuts to serve

PASTE

3 teaspoons gapi (Thai shrimp paste)

16 large dried red chillies, soaked in boiling water for 30 minutes, drained

3 lemongrass stems, white part only, chopped

6 small red Asian shallots, chopped

2.5 cm (1 in) piece fresh galangal, chopped

CURRY POWDER

1 tablespoon cumin seeds

1 tablespoon coriander seeds

1 tablespoon fennel seeds

1 tablespoon black peppercorns

6 whole cloves

1 cinnamon stick, broken

4 blades of mace

3 teaspoons ground turmeric

½ nutmeg, freshly grated

For the paste, place all the ingredients in a food processor and process until a coarse paste forms, adding a little water if necessary. Set aside.

For the curry powder, heat a large, heavy-based frying pan over medium–low heat. Add all the spices, except the turmeric and nutmeg, and dry-fry, shaking the pan often, for 4–5 minutes or until fragrant. Transfer to an electric spice grinder, in batches if necessary, and grind to a fine powder. Stir in the turmeric and nutmeg.

Meanwhile, combine the tamarind pulp with the boiling water in a bowl and stand for 20 minutes. Strain the mixture through a sieve, using your fingers to press down on the solids to extract as much liquid as possible. Discard the solids.

In a large wok over medium heat, brown the pork in the oil for 6–8 minutes. Add the paste, shallots, ginger and curry powder and cook, stirring, for 5–7 minutes or until fragrant. Add the fish sauce, soy sauce, pickled garlic, palm sugar, tamarind liquid and 1.2 litres (41 fl oz) water, or enough to just cover the pork. Bring the mixture to a simmer, reduce the heat to low and simmer for 2 hours or until the pork is very tender. Scatter over the peanuts and serve.

Nonya chicken curry

· SERVES 4–6 AS PART OF A SHARED MEAL ·

Baba Nonyas are the descendants of Chinese immigrants who intermarried with Malays over the fifteenth to seventeenth centuries. Also called Peranakans, some of this group live in Indonesia, although they are mostly associated with the city of Malacca on the Malay Peninsula. They have a rich and singular culture, including their own language. Fusing Chinese and Malaysian ingredients and techniques, Nonya cuisine is typified by complex flavourings, as seen in this elegant curry. Serve with steamed rice.

4 chicken leg quarters

1 quantity Nonya curry paste (see page 23)

1 star anise

4 whole cloves

1 cinnamon stick

80 ml (2½ fl oz/⅓ cup) vegetable oil

3 desiree or other all-purpose potatoes (about 600 g/1 lb 5 oz), washed and quartered

625 ml (21 fl oz/2½ cups) Chicken stock (see page 14)

250 ml (8½ fl oz/1 cup) coconut milk

2 tablespoons shaved palm sugar (jaggery)

sea salt

Chilli sambal (see page 18) to serve

Using a large, sharp knife, cut the chicken leg quarters in half between the joint. Trim any excess skin and fat.

In a large wok or saucepan over medium heat, cook the curry paste and whole spices in the oil, stirring, for about 3 minutes or until fragrant. Add the chicken pieces and potatoes and stir to coat well. Add the stock – it should just cover the mixture, so add extra stock or water as necessary. Bring the mixture to a simmer, cover the wok and cook over medium–low heat for 40 minutes or until the chicken and potatoes are tender.

Add the coconut milk and palm sugar and season to taste with sea salt and freshly ground black pepper. Cook, uncovered, over low heat for another 10 minutes or until the sugar has dissolved. Serve with the chilli sambal.

Squid sambal

· **SERVES 4** ·

Not to be confused with the myriad sambals that make up the family of uber-spicy, saucy accompaniments found throughout Indonesia, Malaysia, Brunei and Singapore, this curry is meaty with squid and makes a great dinner when served with plenty of rice and a stir-fried vegetable or two. It's quite fiery, so tone down the chilli factor if you want. Fresh squid is most definitely the go here – frozen squid is rubbery and gives out water when you cook it, which is most unpleasant. It's not hard to deal with fresh squid. Just remember to cut out the hard beak in the middle of the tentacles, get rid of all the innards and give the tubes a really good rinse after you've gutted them. Serve with Turmeric sticky rice (see page 29).

1 tablespoon tamarind pulp

80 ml (2½ fl oz/⅓ cup) boiling water

2 teaspoons dark soy sauce

2 tablespoons shaved palm sugar (jaggery)

800 g (1 lb 12 oz) whole squid, cleaned

80 ml (2½ fl oz/⅓ cup) vegetable oil

250 g (9 oz) cherry tomatoes, halved

lime cheeks to serve

SPICE PASTE

2 teaspoons belacan (Malaysian shrimp paste)

8 large dried red chillies, soaked in boiling water
    for 30 minutes, drained

2 medium red chillies, chopped

2 teaspoons chopped fresh ginger

1 lemongrass stem, white part only, chopped

10 small red Asian shallots (about 150 g/5½ oz
    in total), chopped

4 garlic cloves, chopped

For the paste, wrap the belacan in foil. Heat a small, heavy-based frying pan over medium heat, add the wrapped belacan then dry-fry for 2 minutes on each side, or until fragrant. Cool and unwrap. Transfer to a food processor with the remaining paste ingredients and process until a smooth paste forms, adding a little water if necessary. Alternatively, use a mortar and pestle. Set aside.

Meanwhile, combine the tamarind pulp with the boiling water in a bowl and stand for 20 minutes. Strain the mixture through a sieve, using your fingers to press down on the solids to extract as much liquid as possible. Discard the solids.

Combine the tamarind liquid with the soy sauce and palm sugar in a bowl and stir until the sugar has dissolved.

Cut the squid into pieces about 4–5 cm (1½–2 in) long and 2.5 cm (1 in) wide. Cut the tentacles in half if large, otherwise leave them whole.

In a large wok over medium–high heat, cook the paste in the oil, stirring constantly, for 1 minute or until fragrant. Add the squid and stir-fry for 3 minutes or until nearly tender then add the tamarind and soy mixture. Cook, stirring, for another 2 minutes or until the liquid boils and the squid is tender.

Transfer the squid to a bowl using a slotted spoon, then boil the mixture in the wok until it is reduced and very thick. Return the squid to the wok with the cherry tomatoes, toss to coat then season to taste with salt and freshly ground black pepper. Serve with the lime cheeks for squeezing over.

Prawn and potato curry

· **SERVES 4** ·

For this Malaysian dish, any type of waxy potato works well. We've gone for kipfler (fingerling) potatoes, as they hold their shape perfectly. We've chosen good-sized tiger or king prawns as there's a bit of cooking going on here – if the prawns you choose are too small, they will overcook. The spices and curry leaves are a nod to Malaysia's Indian influence; the addition of tamarind and coconut gives an extra and exotic edge. This curry is simple and delicious.

300 g (10½ oz) kipfler (fingerling) or other small
   waxy potatoes, scrubbed
1 tablespoon tamarind pulp
80 ml (2½ fl oz/⅓ cup) boiling water
6 red Asian shallots, finely chopped
1 cinnamon stick, broken
handful of curry leaves
60 ml (2 fl oz/¼ cup) vegetable oil
80 ml (2½ fl oz/⅓ cup) coconut milk
1 kg (2 lb 3 oz) large raw tiger or king prawns
   (shrimp), shelled and deveined, tails intact

1 teaspoon fennel seeds
lime halves to serve

SPICE PASTE
6 garlic cloves, chopped
3 cm (1¼ in) piece fresh ginger, finely chopped
3 medium red chillies, chopped
1 teaspoon ground turmeric

For the spice paste, combine all the ingredients in a food processor and process until a smooth paste forms, adding a little water if necessary. Alternatively, use a mortar and pestle. Set aside.

Cook the potatoes in boiling salted water for 15 minutes or until nearly tender then drain well. Cool slightly then cut into 1.5 cm (½ in) pieces.

Meanwhile, combine the tamarind pulp with the boiling water in a bowl and stand for 20 minutes. Strain the mixture through a sieve, using your fingers to press down on the solids to extract as much liquid as possible. Discard the solids.

In a wok over medium–high heat, cook the shallots, cinnamon stick and curry leaves in the oil, stirring, for 3–4 minutes or until the shallots have softened and are light golden. Add the spice paste and cook for another 2 minutes or until fragrant. Add the potatoes and cook, stirring, for 2–3 minutes or until almost cooked through. Add the coconut milk, tamarind liquid and salt and freshly ground black pepper to taste. Bring to a simmer and cook for 8 minutes or until the liquid is very reduced and the oil has separated. Add the prawns and fennel seeds and continue cooking, stirring often, for about 8 minutes or until the prawns are cooked, the potatoes are crisp and golden and the curry is very aromatic.

Turn out onto a platter or into individual bowls and serve with the lime cheeks.

Red duck curry with lychees

· SERVES 4 ·

This dish simply rocks. It's a mild curry featuring the smoothness of coconut milk and the sweetness of lychees. (You can use tinned lychees if fresh aren't available, but the flavour is nowhere near as good.) This recipe is made simpler by buying a barbecued duck from an Asian barbecue shop. Ask them to cut it up for you into bite-sized pieces. Serve this southern Thai–style curry with steamed jasmine rice.

1 quantity Red curry paste (see page 23)
2 tablespoons vegetable oil
1 litre (34 fl oz/4 cups) coconut milk
60 ml (2 fl oz/¼ cup) fish sauce
1 Chinese barbecued duck (available from Asian barbecue shops), cut into 5 cm (2 in) pieces through the bone

450 g (1 lb) fresh lychees, peeled and seeded, or 250 g (9 oz) tinned lychees, drained, juice reserved
250 g (9 oz) cherry tomatoes
handful of Thai basil leaves, coarsely chopped
handful of coriander (cilantro) leaves, coarsely chopped
1 long red chilli, thinly sliced to serve
Thai basil leaves to serve

In a large wok over medium heat, cook the curry paste in the oil for about 5 minutes or until aromatic. Add the coconut milk and fish sauce and bring to a gentle simmer. Add the duck, lychees and reserved juice (or 60 ml/2 fl oz/¼ cup water if using fresh lychees) and simmer for 5–7 minutes.

Remove the wok from the heat and add the cherry tomatoes and herbs. Rest for 5 minutes to soften the tomatoes, then season with salt and freshly ground black pepper. Scatter over the chilli and Thai basil and serve immediately in bowls.

Prawn and omelette curry

· **SERVES 4** ·

The most memorable version of this dish that we ever ate wasn't in Thailand at all, but rather in West Hollywood in LA, at a neighbourhood restaurant called Jitlada. A humble place in a shopping strip and with a huge cult-following, their food is off-the-dial amazing. Don't despair if you can't procure cha om (acacia leaves) – although they can be found in the freezers of specialist Thai grocers. You can substitute very finely shredded English spinach leaves which, though they won't deliver that distinctive, almost medicinal flavour, will still taste great.

1 tablespoon tamarind pulp
80 ml (2½ fl oz/⅓ cup) boiling water
2 tablespoons vegetable oil
1 litre (34 fl oz/4 cups) Chicken stock (see page 14)
60 ml (2 fl oz/¼ cup) fish sauce
12 large raw king prawns (shrimp), peeled and deveined
2½ tablespoons fresh lime juice, or to taste

CURRY PASTE

2 teaspoons belacan (Malaysian shrimp paste)
10 medium dried red chillies, soaked in boiling water
   for 30 minutes, drained

4 medium fresh red chillies, chopped
4 garlic cloves, chopped
4 large red Asian shallots, chopped
1 tablespoon chopped fresh turmeric or 1 teaspoon
   ground turmeric

OMELETTE

110 g (4 oz) frozen thawed cha om (acacia leaves)
5 eggs, very well beaten
2 teaspoons fish sauce
1 tablespoon vegetable oil

For the curry paste, wrap the belacan in foil. Heat a small, heavy-based frying pan over medium heat, add the wrapped belacan then dry-fry for 2 minutes on each side, or until fragrant. Cool and unwrap then transfer to a food processor with the other ingredients and process until a smooth paste forms, adding a little water if necessary. Alternatively, use a mortar and pestle.

Combine the tamarind pulp with the boiling water in a bowl and stand for 20 minutes. Strain the mixture through a sieve, using your fingers to press down on the solids to extract as much liquid as possible. Discard the solids.

For the omelette, use your hands to wring as much liquid from the cha om as possible, then coarsely chop it. Put it in a bowl with the egg and fish sauce and stir to mix well.

In a large, heavy-based, non-stick frying pan over medium–high heat, cook the egg mixture in the oil, swirling to coat the base of the pan evenly. Cook for about 3 minutes or until set on the base and light golden, then carefully invert onto a large plate. Slide the omelette back into the pan, uncooked side down, and cook for another 2 minutes or until firm. Invert onto the large plate and cool. Cut into wedges.

In a saucepan over medium heat, cook the curry paste in the oil, stirring, for 2 minutes or until fragrant. Add the stock, tamarind liquid and fish sauce and bring to a simmer. Season to taste with salt and freshly ground black pepper then add the prawns. Cook over medium–low heat for 3–4 minutes or until the prawns are just cooked through. Stir in the lime juice. Divide the omelette wedges among serving bowls, ladle over the curry and serve.

Beef rendang

· SERVES 6 ·

Rendang was traditionally a ceremonial dish of the west Sumatran Minangkabau people of Indonesia, but it has spread throughout the region and is now associated with Malaysia, Singapore, Brunei and broader Indonesia as well. Rendang should be rather dry, and it does take patience to simmer all the liquid until it has disappeared and all that's left is a pool of oil in which the meat browns, but it's totally worth the effort. Trust us. Rendang is simply one of the most amazing dishes you will ever eat. Serve with steamed rice.

1.25 kg (2 lb 12 oz) beef oyster blade, excess fat trimmed and cut into 3.5 cm (1½ in) pieces

2 tablespoons vegetable oil

2 lemongrass stems, bruised and tied in a knot

1 cinnamon stick

2 star anise

6 cardamom pods, bruised

8 kaffir lime leaves

750 ml (25½ fl oz/3 cups) coconut milk

70 g (2½ oz/⅔ cup) fresh grated or frozen thawed grated coconut, toasted (see page 28)

SPICE PASTE

15 dried red chillies, soaked in boiling water for 30 minutes, drained

4 large brown shallots, chopped

6 garlic cloves, chopped

4 cm (1½ in) piece fresh ginger, chopped

4 cm (1½ in) piece fresh galangal, chopped

6 candlenuts, chopped

1 teaspoon hot paprika

1 teaspoon ground turmeric

½ teaspoon ground cloves

½ teaspoon freshly grated nutmeg

TO SERVE

kecap manis garnished with thinly sliced bird's eye chilli

Chilli sambal (see page 18)

For the spice paste, combine all the ingredients in a food processor and process until a smooth paste forms. Alternatively, use a mortar and pestle.

In a large wok over medium heat, cook the paste and beef in the oil, stirring constantly, for 5 minutes or until fragrant and the meat is well coated. Add the lemongrass, cinnamon stick, star anise, cardamom pods, 6 of the kaffir lime leaves, the coconut milk, half the toasted coconut and enough water to just cover the meat. Bring to a simmer, reduce the heat to low and cook for 3–4 hours, stirring occasionally, or until the meat is tender and the liquid is very reduced.

Increase the heat to medium and continue cooking, stirring often to prevent burning, until the meat browns in the residual oil. Take care that the meat does not fall apart – the mixture should be quite dry.

Transfer the beef to a serving dish or bowl. Scatter over the remaining toasted coconut, and serve with the kecap manis and the chilli sambal.

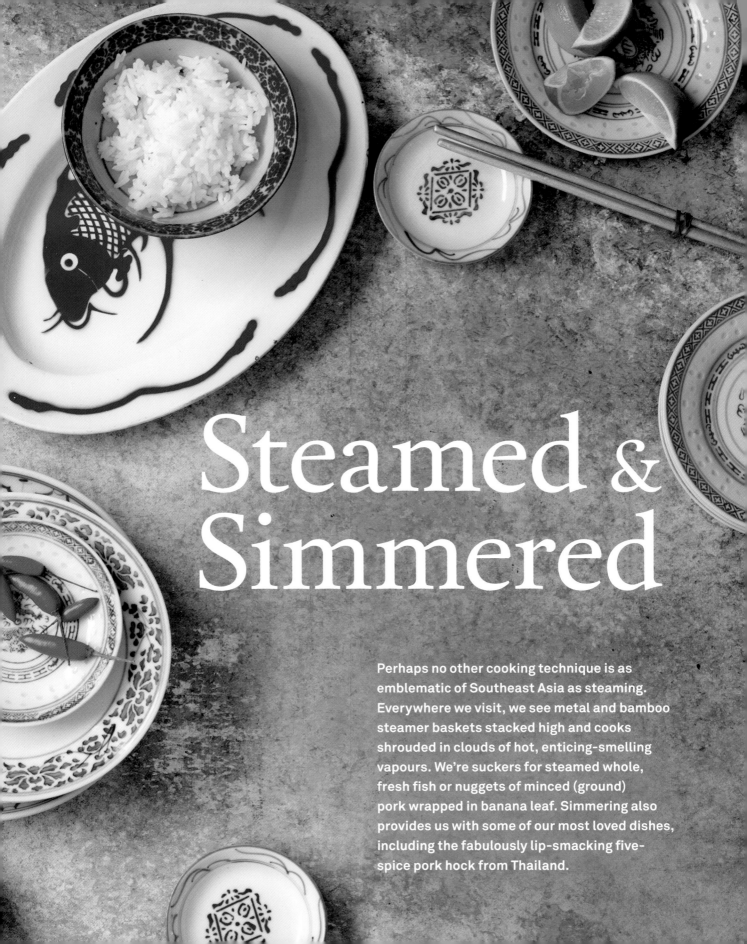

Steamed & Simmered

Perhaps no other cooking technique is as emblematic of Southeast Asia as steaming. Everywhere we visit, we see metal and bamboo steamer baskets stacked high and cooks shrouded in clouds of hot, enticing-smelling vapours. We're suckers for steamed whole, fresh fish or nuggets of minced (ground) pork wrapped in banana leaf. Simmering also provides us with some of our most loved dishes, including the fabulously lip-smacking five-spice pork hock from Thailand.

Fish with lime and chillies

· SERVES 4 ·

Going by the name of *pla neung ma nao,* this steamed dish epitomises the simplest and most elegant aspects of Thai cooking. A few key flavourings and some gentle steam are all that's required – oh, and the freshest whole fish you can lay your hands on! Score the fish flesh through to the bone to encourage even cooking, and stuff the aromatics well into the cavity. This helps the flavour penetrate the fish and creates flavoursome juices in the process. Serve with steamed jasmine rice.

10 garlic cloves, finely chopped

2 bunches of coriander (cilantro) roots and stems, scrubbed and thinly sliced, leaves reserved

8 medium green chillies, thinly sliced

100 ml (3½ fl oz) lime juice

100 ml (3½ fl oz) fish sauce

1 tablespoon shaved palm sugar (jaggery)

1 teaspoon ground white pepper

1 kg (2 lb 3 oz) whole coral trout, snapper or other firm white-fleshed fish

125 ml (4 fl oz/½ cup) Chicken stock (see page 14) or water

lime wedges to serve

In a food processor or blender, process the garlic, coriander roots and stems, and chillies until a coarse paste forms. Add the lime juice, fish sauce, palm sugar and white pepper and stir to combine. Alternatively, use a mortar and pestle.

Put the fish on a chopping board and score each side at 2 cm (¾ in) intervals, making sure you cut through to the bone.

Evenly rub the paste over the fish, ensuring it goes into the cavity and scored sides. Put the fish on a large heatproof plate and pour over the chicken stock.

Put the plated fish in a large steamer basket, place in a deep wok half-filled with boiling water, then cover the wok and steam for 15–18 minutes. Alternatively, cook it in a fish kettle in a 180°C/350°F oven for 30 minutes. You can check if the fish is cooked by piercing the flesh behind its head – it should be opaque and just cooked through.

Carefully transfer the steamed fish to a serving platter. Spoon over the juices, garnish with the reserved coriander leaves and serve with the lime wedges.

See image on pages 136–137.

Balinese pork parcels

· **SERVES 4** ·

Being a non-Muslim enclave, there's no issue with eating pork in Bali, although these parcels can also be made using chicken or even duck. Traditionally the pork would have been chopped by hand. If you use chicken, we'd urge you to hand-chop or coarsely mince (grind) boneless, skinless chicken thighs for the best flavour and texture. If you can't get banana leaves, you can use lightly greased pieces of foil instead.

2 tablespoons vegetable oil, plus extra for brushing
600 g (1 lb 5 oz) minced (ground) pork, not too lean
3–4 large pieces of banana leaf
oil for brushing

1 tablespoon chopped fresh galangal
1 tablespoon chopped fresh ginger
4 red bird's eye chillies, chopped
4 candlenuts, chopped

SPICE PASTE
1 teaspoon trasi (Indonesian shrimp paste)
4 red Asian shallots, chopped
4 garlic cloves, chopped
1 tablespoon chopped fresh turmeric, or 1 teaspoon
  ground turmeric

TO SERVE
Tomato sambal (see page 19)
Lemongrass sambal (see page 18)

For the spice paste, wrap the trasi in foil. Heat a small, heavy-based frying pan over medium heat, add the wrapped trasi then dry-fry for 2 minutes on each side, or until fragrant. Cool and unwrap. Combine with the remaining spice paste ingredients in a food processor and process until a coarse paste forms, adding a little water if necessary. Alternatively, use a mortar and pestle.

In a small saucepan over medium heat, cook the paste in the oil, stirring, for 2–3 minutes or until fragrant. Remove from the heat and cool.

Combine the paste in a bowl with the pork. Using clean hands, knead the mixture to distribute the paste evenly. Season the pork mixture with salt and freshly ground black pepper. Divide into 12 even-sized portions and use your hands to roll each into a log about 8 cm (3¼ in) long.

Using kitchen scissors, trim the tough fibres from the sides of the banana leaf pieces, then cut the leaves to make 12 pieces about 18 cm (7 in) square. Using tongs to hold them, pass each piece over a gas flame until softened and it has turned a darker shade of green. If you don't have gas, blanch them in boiling water for 2 minutes or until they soften. Drain and dry.

Put the leaves, shiny side down, on a work surface and lightly brush each with oil. Put a log of the pork mixture on each, diagonally, then bring the corners of the leaf over the meat. Roll the log up in the leaf then tie using kitchen string, or use a toothpick to secure.

Bring a steamer to the boil, add the rolls and cook for 12 minutes, covered, or until cooked through. Remove the pork logs from the banana leaf pieces and serve with the tomato sambal and lemongrass sambal.

Pork and lettuce wraps

· SERVES 4–6 ·

This is one of those easy dishes, designed for informal, help-yourself dining. What this Cambodian-inspired dish lacks in prettiness, it more than compensates for in flavour. You can use pork neck instead of belly, if you prefer – cook very gently for 3½ hours.

1 piece of pork belly (about 1 kg /2 lb 3 oz), excess fat trimmed

2½ tablespoons fish sauce

1 lemongrass stem, bruised and tied in a knot

175 g (6 oz) dried thin rice noodles

1 large butter lettuce, leaves separated, washed and dried

1 carrot, peeled and shredded into fine ribbons or cut into matchsticks

1 jicama, peeled and shredded into fine ribbons or cut into matchsticks

2 Lebanese (short) cucumbers, shredded into fine ribbons or cut into matchsticks

200 g (7 oz) mung bean sprouts

large handful each of coriander sprigs, mint leaves and Thai basil leaves

2 large fresh red chillies, thinly sliced

PINEAPPLE PEANUT SAUCE

2½ teaspoons tamarind pulp

60 ml (2 fl oz/¼ cup) boiling water

2 garlic cloves, chopped

1 lemongrass stem, white part only, chopped

2 large red Asian shallots, finely chopped

1½ tablespoons vegetable oil

450 g (1 lb) fresh pineapple, peeled, cored, trimmed and finely chopped

1 tablespoon shaved palm sugar (jaggery)

1 tablespoon lime juice

1 tablespoon fish sauce

80 g (2¾ oz/½ cup) roasted unsalted peanuts

Put the pork belly in a saucepan over medium–low heat with the fish sauce, lemongrass and enough cold water to cover. Bring the liquid slowly to just below a gentle simmer and cook over very low heat for about 2½ hours or until the pork is tender and cooked through. Cool the meat in the liquid until either warm or room temperature.

Meanwhile, for the pineapple peanut sauce, combine the tamarind pulp with the boiling water in a bowl and stand for 20 minutes. Strain the mixture through a sieve, using your fingers to press down on the solids to extract as much liquid as possible. Discard the solids.

Combine the garlic, lemongrass and shallots in a food processor and process until finely chopped. Alternatively, use a mortar and pestle.

In a small saucepan over medium heat, cook the garlic mixture in the oil, stirring often, for 3 minutes or until fragrant and it no longer smells raw. Add the pineapple, 170 ml (5½ fl oz/⅔ cup) water, the tamarind liquid, sugar, lime juice and fish sauce. Bring to a simmer, stirring until the palm sugar has dissolved. Cover and cook over low heat for 5–6 minutes or until the pineapple has softened.

Finely chop the peanuts in a food processor and add them to the sauce, stirring to combine well. Bring to a simmer and cook for 1–2 minutes, adding a little more lime juice or fish sauce to taste, and a little more water if the sauce is too thick (it will thicken on standing). Transfer to a serving bowl.

Soak and cook the rice noodles according to the packet instructions, then drain well and place in a serving bowl. Very finely slice the pork and place in another bowl. Place the lettuce leaves, vegetables, sprouts, herbs and chillies on a large platter. Serve immediately with the pineapple peanut sauce.

Caramel galangal salmon

· SERVES 4–6 AS PART OF A SHARED MEAL ·

Vietnam has some unique ingredients and techniques in its huge culinary repertoire, including the use of dark, caramelised sugar in simmered dishes. We love this salmon recipe and it's so simple and quick to put together. You can make the caramel sauce a few hours in advance, if you like, and then cook the salmon at the very end. We also like to make a version of this dish with french-trimmed chicken legs instead of the fish, and loads of julienned fresh ginger. Serve with steamed rice and bok choy.

800 g (1 lb 12 oz) salmon fillets or ocean trout, skin on
90 g (3 oz) caster (superfine) sugar
125 ml (4 fl oz/½ cup) coconut water, or more if necessary
2½ tablespoons fish sauce
1 tablespoon oyster sauce

2 garlic cloves, thinly sliced
4 cm (1½ in) piece fresh galangal, cut into fine matchsticks
2 red bird's eye chillies, thinly sliced, to serve

Remove any pin bones from the salmon, then cut the fish into 4–5 cm (1½–2 in) pieces. Set aside.

Combine the sugar with 2½ tablespoons water in a large, deep frying pan over medium heat. Cook, without stirring, for about 3 minutes or until the sugar has dissolved and the mixture is boiling. Cook for another 5–6 minutes or until the mixture has thickened and smells caramelised. Be careful as the mixture will now be very hot!

Working quickly, remove the pan from the heat, add the coconut water and fish sauce, taking care as the mixture will spit. Add the oyster sauce, garlic and galangal, swirling the pan to combine everything, then return the pan to the heat and simmer for 2 minutes to allow the flavours to develop.

Add the fish to the pan, skin side up, in a single layer if possible. Bring the caramel mixture to a simmer and cook, turning the fish once during cooking time, for 6–7 minutes or until just cooked through. Add a little extra coconut water if the sauce reduces too quickly.

Spoon the sauce over the fish and serve with the sliced chillies on the side.

Five-spice pork

· SERVES 6 ·

Khao kha moo, as the Thai people call this, is a dish commonly sold by local street vendors. The sweetness from the palm sugar is offset by the bracing, vinegary dipping sauce. We've read about and sampled many variations of this dish, even some with Coca-Cola added to the stewing liquid. We've opted to keep things simple here – this version reminds us of one we like from Chiang Mai. Choose fresh, meaty pork hocks, not the cured or smoked variety. Serve with steamed jasmine rice.

8 garlic cloves, chopped

8 coriander (cilantro) roots, scrubbed and chopped,
   or 1 tablespoon ground coriander

1½ teaspoons ground white pepper

3 x 800 g (1 lb 12 oz) pork hocks

100 ml (3 ½ fl oz) vegetable oil

1 cinnamon stick

3 star anise

125 ml (4 fl oz/½ cup) light soy sauce

80 ml (2½ fl oz/⅓ cup) dark soy sauce

125 g (4½ oz) shaved palm sugar (jaggery)

1 teaspoon five-spice powder

5 pandan leaves, bruised and tied in a bundle

650 g (1 lb 7 oz) pickled mustard greens (available
   from Asian supermarkets), drained

6 hard-boiled eggs, peeled

Vinegar chilli sauce (page 15) to serve

Combine the garlic, coriander and pepper in a food processor and process until a coarse paste forms. Alternatively, use a mortar and pestle.

In a large frying pan over medium heat, cook the pork hocks in 60 ml (2 fl oz/¼ cup) of the oil, in batches if necessary, turning occasionally, for 10–12 minutes or until browned all over. Transfer to a large bowl.

Heat the remaining oil in a large saucepan over medium heat. Add the paste to the pan and cook, stirring constantly, for 1 minute or until fragrant. Add the pork hocks to the pan along with the cinnamon stick, star anise, soy sauces, palm sugar, five-spice powder, pandan leaves and enough water to just cover the pork. Bring to a simmer, skimming any impurities that rise to the surface, and cook over low heat for 3 hours or until the meat is tender. Add a little water if necessary to keep the hocks covered.

Soak the mustard greens in water for 15 minutes and drain well, pressing down on the greens to extract as much liquid as possible.

Add the mustard greens and eggs to the pan and cook for another 30 minutes or until the meat is very tender and the eggs are coloured.

Remove the pork from the liquid and pull the meat from the bones, taking care as it will be hot.

Slice the meat, then divide among plates with the eggs and mustard greens. Ladle a little of the cooking liquid over and serve with the vinegar chilli sauce for dipping.

Opor ayam

· **SERVES 4** ·

This classic central Javanese chicken stew is good to serve to non-chilli-loving friends as, although it contains plenty of spices, it isn't hot. In Java it's popular during Eid ul-fitr, the feast to celebrate the end of Ramadan. It's also served as part of one of our favourite dishes of all time, *gudeg*, which you find in Yogyakarta. It's an incredibly sweet stew of young jackfruit, served for breakfast with *opor ayam* and a sambal of beef skin, among other things.

1 x 1.8 kg (4 lb) chicken
60 ml (2 fl oz/¼ cup) vegetable oil
400 ml (13½ fl oz) coconut milk
375 ml (12½ fl oz/1½ cups) Chicken stock (see page 14) or water
1 lemongrass stem, bruised and tied in a knot
8 kaffir lime leaves, bruised
6 whole cloves
1 cinnamon stick
2 star anise
large pinch of freshly grated nutmeg
1 tablespoon shaved palm sugar (jaggery)
Fried shallots (see page 26) to garnish
Roasted coconut and peanuts (see page 21) to garnish

PASTE
1 tablespoon ground coriander
1½ teaspoons ground cumin
1 teaspoon ground white pepper
4 garlic cloves, chopped
8 red Asian shallots, chopped
6 candlenuts, chopped
1½ tablespoons chopped fresh galangal
1 tablespoon trasi (Indonesian shrimp paste)

For the paste, combine all the ingredients in a food processor and process until a coarse paste forms. Alternatively, use a mortar and pestle.

Using a large, sharp knife, cut the chicken through the bone between the leg and the body to remove the leg quarters. Put the remaining chicken on a chopping board, breast side up, and cut through either side of the backbone. Remove the backbone and discard. Put the chicken, skin side down, on the board, and cut in half down the breast bone. You should have 4 pieces of chicken.

Add the oil to a large wok over medium–high heat, swirling to coat the surface. Add the chicken and cook for about 8 minutes, turning once, until light golden all over. Transfer to a plate.

Pour out all but 2 tablespoons of the oil from the wok. Reduce the heat to medium, add the paste and cook, stirring, for 3 minutes or until fragrant. Add the coconut milk, stock, lemongrass, kaffir lime leaves, spices and palm sugar and return the chicken to the wok – the chicken will not be completely covered. Bring the mixture to a gentle simmer and cook over low heat for about 45 minutes or until tender, turning the chicken halfway through. Season well with salt and freshly ground black pepper and serve garnished with the fried shallots and roasted coconut and peanuts.

Orange and ginger duck

· SERVES 4 ·

The French have influenced Vietnam since their colonisation of the country in the mid-nineteenth century, and this dish has its origins firmly in the classic French dish *canard à l'orange*. The key to not drying out any meat that is slow-simmered like this, is to maintain a low temperature – the bubbles should be just breaking the surface. Get this right and the meat will fall off the bone. Serve with steamed rice.

1 x 2.25 kg (5 lb) duck
2 tablespoons vegetable oil
5 cm (2 in) piece fresh ginger, cut into fine matchsticks
4 garlic cloves, crushed
6 small dried red chillies
2 lemongrass stems, bruised and tied in a knot
750 ml (25½ fl oz/3 cups) freshly squeezed orange juice, plus extra if needed
80 ml (2½ fl oz/⅓ cup) lime juice
60 ml (2 fl oz/¼ cup) fish sauce
2 tablespoons shaved palm sugar (jaggery)

2 star anise
1 cinnamon stick
2 oranges
1 tablespoon cornflour (cornstarch)

TO SERVE
spring onions (scallions), thinly sliced diagonally
coriander (cilantro) sprigs
sesame oil
toasted sesame seeds

Using a large, sharp knife, cut the duck through the bone between the leg and the body to remove the leg quarters. Cut each leg quarter into 2 pieces so you have 2 thighs and 2 drumsticks. Put the remaining duck on a chopping board, breast side up. Cut through either side of the backbone, and remove the backbone. Put the duck, skin side down, on the board, and cut in half down the breast bone. Cut each breast into 2 pieces crossways. You should have 8 pieces of duck.

In a large wok over medium heat, cook the duck pieces in the oil, turning occasionally, for 15–20 minutes or until deep golden and much of the fat has rendered out. Transfer the duck to a bowl and set aside.

Pour all but 2 tablespoons of fat from the pan. Add the ginger, garlic and chillies and cook, stirring, for 2–3 minutes or until fragrant. Return the duck to the wok with the lemongrass, orange juice and lime juice, fish sauce, palm sugar, star anise and cinnamon stick, adding a little more orange juice if necessary so the duck is just covered. Season well with salt and freshly ground black pepper to taste. Bring to a simmer then reduce the heat to low. Cook the duck, partially covered, for 60–70 minutes, occasionally skimming any impurities that rise to the surface, or until the duck is very tender. Discard the lemongrass, remove the duck pieces and transfer them to a bowl.

Meanwhile, using a small, sharp knife, peel the oranges, taking care to remove all the white pith. Slice the oranges thinly.

Mix the cornflour with 2 tablespoons water in a bowl to form a smooth paste. Bring the cooking liquid in the pan to a simmer then, stirring constantly, add the cornflour mixture and cook until the liquid boils and thickens. Return the duck to the sauce along with the orange slices to heat through.

Divide the duck and sauce among large bowls, then scatter over handfuls of the spring onion slices, coriander and some orange slices. Drizzle with sesame oil, sprinkle over the sesame seeds and serve.

Rich spice-braised beef

· **SERVES 4–6** ·

Called *bo kho*, this soothing Vietnamese beef braise is quite French in its simplicity, technique and overall elegance, which is hardly surprising, given the French influence on Vietnamese cuisine. Versions of this recipe call for the use of annatto oil, largely for colour, and the addition of beef tendons too. We've opted not to add these, but feel free to sauté the beef in annatto oil (which you can buy at Asian and Latin supermarkets) and to add 2–3 sliced beef tendons to the mixture at the start of cooking. Serve with a baguette or steamed jasmine rice, for mopping up the delicious sauce.

60 ml (2 fl oz/¼ cup) fish sauce

2½ tablespoons shaved palm sugar (jaggery)

¼ teaspoon five-spice powder

1 kg (2 lb 3 oz) chuck or boneless shin beef, trimmed and cut into 4 cm (1½ in) pieces

plain (all-purpose) flour for dusting

80 ml (2½ fl oz/⅓ cup) vegetable oil

2 large onions, sliced

3 garlic cloves, crushed

3 cm (1¼ in) piece fresh ginger, cut into fine matchsticks

2 tablespoons tomato paste (concentrated purée)

2 tablespoons dark soy sauce

2 star anise

1 cinnamon stick

6 small dried red chillies

1 lemongrass stem, bruised

600 ml (20½ fl oz) coconut water or Chicken stock (see page 14)

450 g (1 lb) carrots (about 4), sliced

Thai basil leaves to serve

Combine 2 tablespoons of the fish sauce with the palm sugar, five-spice powder and beef in a large bowl, and toss to coat the meat. Cover tightly with plastic wrap and refrigerate for 2 hours for the flavours to develop.

Drain the meat well, reserving the marinade, and lightly dust with flour.

In a non-stick frying pan or large wok over medium–high heat, cook the meat in 2 tablespoons of the oil, in batches, for 5 minutes, turning often until browned all over. Transfer to a saucepan and wipe the frying pan clean.

Increase the heat to high and cook the onion, garlic and ginger in the frying pan in the remaining oil for 2 minutes or until lightly browned. Add to the meat in the saucepan, then stir in the tomato paste, soy sauce, remaining fish sauce, spices, lemongrass, coconut water, carrots and reserved marinade, adding a little water to just cover the meat if necessary.

Bring the mixture slowly to a simmer over medium heat, skimming any impurities that rise to the surface, and cook over low heat for 1 hour 10 minutes or until the meat is very tender. Discard the lemongrass and serve with the Thai basil leaves scattered over.

Coconut ginger spatchcock

· SERVES 6 ·

Drinking the contents of a freshly opened young coconut on a hot, steamy Cambodian, Thai or Vietnamese day has saved our parched bacon on many an occasion. We also love cooking with it. While the spatchcock here might not be wholly traditional (feel free to use chicken pieces if you prefer), the gentle flavour combination of ginger and pepper is classic Vietnamese. Serve with rice and steamed greens.

4 x 450 g (1 lb) spatchcocks (poussins)
60 ml (2 fl oz/¼ cup) vegetable oil
4 garlic cloves, very thinly sliced
4 cm (1½ in) piece fresh ginger, cut into
   very fine matchsticks
1 litre (34 fl oz/4 cups) coconut water, plus extra
   if necessary

2½ tablespoons fish sauce
1½ tablespoons caster (superfine) sugar
1½ teaspoons freshly ground black pepper
coriander (cilantro) sprigs to garnish
thinly sliced red bird's eye chillies to serve

Working with one at a time, put the spatchcocks, breast side up, on a chopping board. Using a large, sharp knife, cut down each side of the backbone and remove the backbone. Discard. Turn each spatchcock over, skin side down, then cut through the breastbone. Remove the legs by cutting through the thigh joint nearest the body. You should have 16 pieces of spatchcock in total.

Heat half the oil in a large frying pan over medium heat, add the spatchcock pieces, in batches if necessary, and cook, turning once, for 6 minutes or until lightly browned on both sides. Transfer to a bowl.

In a wok or large saucepan over medium heat, cook the garlic and ginger in the remaining oil, stirring, for 3–4 minutes or until fragrant and softened. Add the spatchcock pieces and all the remaining ingredients, except the coriander and chilli, reduce the heat to medium–low and bring to a gentle simmer. Add a little extra coconut water or water to just cover the spatchcock if necessary. Cook for 20 minutes or until the spatchcock is cooked through.

Remove the spatchcock pieces from the liquid and bring the liquid to the boil. Cook over high heat for 10 minutes or until the liquid has reduced and thickened slightly. Return the spatchcock to the wok and toss to coat well. Serve immediately with the coriander scattered over and the sliced chilli on the side.

Sour chicken and eggplant stew

· **SERVES 4** ·

Sour stews, called *samlor*, are popular in Cambodia and are based around a variety of ingredients, such as vegetables, fish, chicken and beef. They are spiked with plenty of herbs and spices as well as prahok (fermented fish paste), one of the country's defining flavours. Serve with steamed rice.

2 tablespoons prahok (fermented fish paste)

2 tablespoons tamarind pulp

190 ml (6½ fl oz/¾ cup) boiling water

2½ tablespoons vegetable oil

2½ tablespoons fish sauce, plus extra to serve

1½ tablespoons shaved palm sugar (jaggery)

625 ml (21 fl oz/2½ cups) Chicken stock (see page 14)

6 kaffir lime leaves, bruised

¼ cabbage, (about 400 g/14 oz), trimmed, leaves cut into 5 cm (2 in) pieces

1 bunch of snake (yard-long) beans, trimmed and cut into 3 cm (1¼ in) chunks

5 apple eggplants (aubergines) (about 250 g/9 oz in total), trimmed and thinly sliced

400 g (14 oz) boneless, skinless chicken breasts (about 2), cut into 1.5 cm (½ in) thick slices

Thai basil leaves to serve

PASTE

2.5 cm (1 in) piece fresh galangal, chopped

3 large brown shallots, chopped

4 garlic cloves, chopped

1 tablespoon chopped fresh turmeric or 1 teaspoon ground turmeric

2 lemongrass stems, white part only, chopped

For the paste, combine all the ingredients in a food processor and process until a coarse paste forms, adding a little water if necessary. Alternatively, use a mortar and pestle.

Combine the prahok and 250 ml (8½ fl oz/1 cup) water in a saucepan over medium–low heat and bring to a simmer. Cook for 5 minutes, then strain the mixture, pressing down on the solids in the sieve with the back of a spoon to extract as much liquid as possible. Discard the solids.

Combine the tamarind pulp with the boiling water in a bowl and stand for 20 minutes. Strain the mixture through a sieve, using your fingers to press down on the solids to extract as much liquid as possible. Discard the solids.

In a saucepan over medium heat, cook the paste in the oil, stirring, for 2–3 minutes or until fragrant. Add the prahok liquid, tamarind liquid, fish sauce, palm sugar, stock and kaffir lime leaves and bring to a simmer. Add the cabbage, cover and cook for 3 minutes or until slightly softened. Add the beans, eggplant and chicken, cover and cook over low heat for 8 minutes or until the vegetables have softened a little (the eggplant should not be completely soft) and the chicken is cooked through – do not let the mixture simmer too fast or the chicken will be dry. Season well with freshly ground black pepper and extra fish sauce to taste. Serve with the Thai basil on the side for scattering over.

Fried

Nothing, simply nothing, beats the sound of a hissing wok as tasty morsels are fried and crisped-up to golden, crunchy deliciousness in lakes of bubbling oil. Well, nothing perhaps except eating those morsels once they're done! Cooking in oil makes everything taste incredible and, if you do it properly – always check the temperature and always use fresh oil – the results are never, ever greasy. Artful frying seals in moisture and flavour, and each and every recipe here has been chosen with flavour and juiciness very firmly in mind.

Chicken wings with green mango salad

· SERVES 4 ·

In the West we tend to favour cuts of meat that come without the perceived challenges of skin, bones and connective tissue. But these are the very elements that make wings so darned delicious! It's such a satisfying experience, gnawing the succulent flesh off a grilled or fried wing, taking in all the lip-smacking skin, tendon and lush bits of fat. In Southeast Asia they have no such qualms about 'lesser' cuts, particularly in Cambodia, where we've eaten many a fine wing. The green mango salad is wonderful but not essential.

60 ml (2 fl oz/¼ cup) fish sauce

5 garlic cloves, crushed

2 teaspoons caster (superfine) sugar

1½ teaspoons ground white pepper

8 chicken wings (about 1.4 kg/3 lb 1 oz),
   wing tips trimmed

vegetable oil for deep-frying

rice flour for coating

PALM SUGAR SAUCE

2½ tablespoons shaved palm sugar (jaggery)

1 tablespoon light soy sauce

1 tablespoon oyster sauce

1 tablespoon Sriracha sauce

GREEN MANGO SALAD

1½ tablespoons shaved palm sugar (jaggery)

2 tablespoons lime juice

2 tablespoons rice vinegar

2 garlic cloves, crushed

3 teaspoons sesame oil

3 green mangoes (about 750 g/1 lb 11 oz in total), flesh
   shredded into fine ribbons or cut into matchsticks

handful of torn Thai basil leaves

handful of torn coriander (cilantro) leaves

2 medium red chillies, sliced

50 g (1¾ oz/⅓ cup) chopped roasted cashew nuts

150 g (5½ oz) mung bean sprouts (optional)

1 red onion, thinly sliced

Combine the fish sauce, garlic, sugar and pepper in a large bowl. Add the chicken wings and, using your hands, rub the marinade all over the chicken. Cover with plastic wrap and refrigerate for 8 hours or overnight, turning the wings occasionally.

For the palm sugar sauce, combine the palm sugar with 2½ tablespoons water in a small saucepan over low heat, and cook, stirring, until the sugar has dissolved. Add the remaining ingredients and cook, stirring, until smooth. Remove from the heat and set aside.

For the green mango salad, in a small bowl whisk together the palm sugar, lime juice, rice vinegar, garlic and sesame oil. Combine the mango in a large bowl with the herbs, chillies, cashew nuts, mung bean sprouts, if using, and the sliced onion. Set aside.

Remove the chicken from the marinade and drain well, discarding the marinade. Heat enough oil for deep-frying in a large saucepan until it reaches 180°C (350°F), or until a cube of bread turns golden in 15 seconds. Dust the chicken in the rice flour, making sure it is well coated all over. Deep-fry the chicken, in batches if necessary, for 10 minutes or until deep golden and cooked through. Transfer to a plate lined with paper towel to drain any excess oil. Serve with the palm sugar sauce for drizzling over and the green mango salad.

See image on pages 160–161.

Lemongrass fried chicken

· **SERVES 4** ·

Ga xao xa ot, as this dish is called in Vietnamese, is as perfect a combination of lemongrass and chicken as you're ever likely to find. We've opted for thigh meat, as it's less likely to dry out than leaner breast meat, but feel free to use breast if you prefer. Whatever you do, don't rush the marinating, as it needs time to do its thing! The resulting dish is a beautiful mixture of sweet caramel, lemongrass and chilli, but don't forget the limes to squeeze over at the end, which help cut through the richness. Serve with steamed jasmine rice.

2 lemongrass stems, white part only, chopped, plus extra for garnish

5 small red Asian shallots, chopped

5 garlic cloves, finely chopped

1½ tablespoons Vietnamese curry powder

80 g (2¾ oz/⅓ cup) caster (superfine) sugar

1 teaspoon freshly ground black pepper

60 ml (2 fl oz/¼ cup) fish sauce

900 g (2 lb) boneless, skinless chicken thighs

60 ml (2 fl oz/¼ cup) vegetable oil

3 medium red chillies, thinly sliced

2 limes, halved, to serve

Combine the lemongrass, shallots, garlic, curry powder, 2 teaspoons of the sugar, the pepper and fish sauce in a food processor and process until a coarse paste forms. Alternatively, use a mortar and pestle. Combine with the chicken in a bowl and, using your hands, toss to coat the chicken well. Cover the bowl with plastic wrap and refrigerate for 3–8 hours.

Remove the chicken from the refrigerator and bring to room temperature.

Meanwhile, combine the remaining sugar with 2 tablespoons water in a small saucepan and slowly bring to a simmer over medium–high heat. Cook for about 5 minutes or until a deep caramel colour. Remove from the heat and, taking care as the mixture will spit, add 2 tablespoons water, swirling the pan to combine well. Set aside.

Drain the chicken well, reserving any liquid and wiping any excess solids off the chicken. In a large wok over medium–high heat, stir-fry the chicken in the oil, in 2 batches, for 12 minutes or until the chicken is cooked through and golden. Return all the chicken to the wok, add the reserved liquid, the caramel and chillies and toss to combine well. Continue cooking until the chicken is heated through and the liquid is very reduced. Serve with the lime halves to squeeze over.

Pepper and curry leaf crab

· **SERVES 4–6** ·

Malaysia is nirvana for the food lover. It's at the confluence of so many culinary threads – Indian, Chinese, Portuguese, Thai and Indonesian. The flavours are bold, spicy and rich and are infused into diverse cooking styles. It's possibly the ultimate 'fusion' cuisine. One of the best (and loveliest) spots to contemplate this first hand is the historic city of Malacca, where this dish loosely hails from. If we were eating this in Malacca, we'd probably wash it down with a fresh coconut milkshake from Klebang, on Jalan Klebang Besar.

2½ tablespoons dried shrimp

2 tablespoons fermented black beans, rinsed well

2½ tablespoons light soy sauce

1 tablespoon dark soy sauce

1 tablespoon caster (superfine) sugar

4 raw blue swimmer crabs or other large crabs

125 ml (4 fl oz/½ cup) vegetable oil

6 red Asian shallots, thinly sliced

4 garlic cloves, crushed

2 tablespoons black peppercorns, crushed

large handful of fresh curry leaves plus extra to garnish

30 g (1 oz) butter

Finely grind the dried shrimp to a powder in an electric spice grinder. Set aside.

Combine the fermented black beans, soy sauces, sugar and 60 ml (2 fl oz/¼ cup) water in a bowl and set aside.

To prepare the crabs, working with one at a time, turn the crab over so the underside is facing you. Using your fingers, lift the tail flap and pull the outer shell away from the body from the point under the flap. Discard that shell.

Cut each crab into quarters using a large, heavy knife. Pull out and discard any feathery gills from the crab pieces, then rinse lightly under cold running water. Dry the crabs on paper towel.

In a large wok over medium–high heat, stir-fry the crab quarters in the oil, in 2 batches, for 3–4 minutes or until half cooked. Transfer to a large bowl using a slotted spoon.

Discard all but 2 tablespoons of the oil from the wok. Add the shallots, garlic, peppercorns and curry leaves and stir-fry for 1–2 minutes or until fragrant. Add the dried shrimp powder and return the crab to the wok with the butter and the fermented black bean mixture. Cover the wok with a lid and cook, turning the crab once, for 5 minutes or until the crab is cooked through.

Serve immediately with fresh curry leaves scattered over the top.

Tofu with peanut sauce

· SERVES 4 AS A LIGHT MEAL OR AS PART OF A SHARED MEAL ·

The Indonesians, particularly on the island of Java, excel at cooking tempeh and tofu. Often these delicious (and cheap) staples are served in curries, or they are deep-fried, as in this recipe. Tofu particularly, because its own flavour is relatively bland, takes on other flavours readily and, if you always think of it as a wholly vegetarian food, think again. This dish, with its peanutty dressing, is gutsy and filling and oh so delicious. It will win over even the most avowed red meat eater.

200 g (7 oz) mung bean sprouts

4 Lebanese (short) cucumbers (about 500 g/1 lb 2 oz in total), trimmed and cut into batons

peanut oil for deep-frying

600 g (1 lb 5 oz) firm tofu

rice flour for coating

50 g (1¾ oz/⅓ cup) roasted unsalted peanuts, crushed

PEANUT SAUCE

2½ tablespoons shaved palm sugar (jaggery)

2½ tablespoons tamarind pulp

250 ml (8½ fl oz/1 cup) boiling water

5 red bird's eye chillies, chopped

3 garlic cloves, chopped

160 g (5½ oz/1 cup) roasted unsalted peanuts, chopped

1 tablespoon kecap manis

1 tablespoon lime juice

For the peanut sauce, put the sugar in a small saucepan over medium heat with 125 ml (4 fl oz/½ cup) water and heat until the sugar has dissolved. Remove from the heat.

Meanwhile, combine the tamarind pulp with the boiling water in a bowl and stand for 20 minutes. Strain the mixture through a sieve, using your fingers to press down on the solids to extract as much liquid as possible. Discard the solids.

Combine the chillies and garlic in a food processor and process until a smooth paste forms. Add the peanuts, tamarind liquid, palm sugar mixture and kecap manis and process until a chunky sauce forms, adding a little water if necessary – there should be a little texture in the peanuts. Transfer the mixture to a small saucepan and bring to a simmer over medium–low heat. Cook, stirring often, over low heat for 4–5 minutes, until the flavours develop. Add a little more water if the mixture becomes too thick. Stir in the lime juice and remove from the heat.

Toss the mung bean sprouts and cucumber in a bowl then divide among plates or place on a large platter.

Heat enough peanut oil for deep-frying in a large saucepan or wok to 170°C (340°F), or until a cube of bread turns golden in 20 seconds.

Meanwhile cut the tofu into pieces about 5 x 2.5 cm (2 x 1 in) and toss them in the rice flour to coat, shaking off any excess flour. Fry the tofu pieces, in batches, for 4–5 minutes or until golden and crisp. Place them on top of the vegetables, pour over the sauce, scatter over the crushed peanuts and serve.

Fried Nonya chicken

· SERVES 4 ·

Nothing beats good fried chicken! On our travels, we quickly learnt that Southeast Asian cooks are master chicken-friers. Called *inche kabin* in Malaysia, this dish has a marinade that packs some flavour. You'll note the appearance of mustard and worcestershire sauce – a hang-over from the British colonial times and further reinforcing Malaysia as the true home of 'fusion' cuisine. Serve with steamed rice and Vegetable pickle salad (see page 81).

1 x 1.8 kg (4 lb) chicken
vegetable oil for frying

PASTE

1 cinnamon stick, roughly broken
6 dried red chillies, stem ends trimmed
1 tablespoon coriander seeds
2½ teaspoons cumin seeds
2 teaspoons fennel seeds
1 teaspoon black peppercorns
4 whole cloves
1 tablespoon chopped fresh turmeric
   or 1 teaspoon ground turmeric

150 ml (5 fl oz) coconut milk
6 small red Asian shallots, chopped
1 tablespoon shaved palm sugar (jaggery)

SAUCE

1 teaspoon hot mustard powder
60 ml (2 fl oz/¼ cup) worcestershire sauce
3 teaspoons shaved palm sugar (jaggery)
3 teaspoons lime juice
2 teaspoons light soy sauce
3 red bird's eye chillies, thinly sliced

Using a large, sharp knife, cut the chicken down either side of the backbone then discard the backbone or reserve it for stock. Cut through the joint between the body and thigh to remove the leg quarters, then cut through the leg joint to remove the drumsticks. Cut each thigh in half through the bone. Put the remaining chicken on the board, skin side down, then cut down the breast bone to cut in half. Remove the wings. Cut the breasts in half through the bone, trimming any excess bones along the edge. You should have 12 pieces of chicken. Transfer the chicken pieces to a large bowl.

For the paste, put the whole spices in an electric spice grinder and grind to a coarse powder. Transfer to a food processor with the remaining paste ingredients and process until a coarse paste forms. Alternatively, use a mortar and pestle.

Combine the paste with the chicken in the bowl, using your hands to toss the chicken in the mixture to coat well. Cover the bowl with plastic wrap and refrigerate for 3–4 hours or overnight.

For the sauce, combine the mustard powder with 2–3 teaspoons water or just enough to make a smooth paste. Add the remaining ingredients, except the chillies, and whisk until the sugar has dissolved. Stir in the chillies.

Bring the chicken to room temperature and remove it from the marinade. Dry the chicken well on paper towel.

Heat the oil in a wok or large saucepan until it reaches 180°C (350°F), or until a cube of bread turns golden in 15 seconds. Fry the chicken, in batches, for 12 minutes or until deep golden and cooked through. Transfer the chicken to a plate lined with paper towel to drain any excess oil. Serve the chicken with the sauce for dipping.

FRIED

Cha ca

· SERVES 4 ·

It's every Hanoi first-timer's rite of passage – a dinner at the gorgeous, rickety Cha Ca La Vong in the Old Quarter. Their raison d'etre is to serve just one dish – *cha ca*. Pieces of local Red River fish (carp or catfish) are marinated with turmeric then fried at the table with heaps of dill and spring onion and served over rice noodles with peanuts and a dipping sauce (*mam tom tong*).

3 teaspoons chopped fresh ginger

3 red Asian shallots, chopped

4 garlic cloves, chopped

2¾ teaspoons ground turmeric

60 ml (2 fl oz/¼ cup) fish sauce

750 g (1 lb 11 oz) skinless blue eye cod or other firm white-fleshed fish fillets, cut into 4 cm (1½ in) pieces

1 teaspoon freshly ground black pepper

375 g (13 oz) dried thin rice-stick noodles

90 g (3 oz/½ cup) rice flour

1 teaspoon salt

80 ml (2½ fl oz/⅓ cup) vegetable oil, plus extra if necessary

8 spring onions (scallions), trimmed and cut into 4 cm (1½ in) pieces plus extra, finely sliced, to garnish

1 onion, halved and sliced

2 bunches of dill, coarsely torn

160 g (5½ oz/1 cup) roasted unsalted peanuts, coarsely chopped

SAUCE

80 ml (2½ fl oz/⅓ cup) mam nem (Vietnamese fermented shrimp sauce)

3 garlic cloves, crushed

1 tablespoon caster (superfine) sugar

1 lemongrass stem, white part only, finely chopped

2 tablespoons fish sauce

2 tablespoons lime juice

2 medium red chillies, finely chopped

95 g (3¼ oz/½ cup) very finely chopped fresh pineapple flesh

Combine the ginger, shallots, garlic, 2 teaspoons of the turmeric and fish sauce in a food processor and process until a coarse paste forms.

Put the fish in a bowl with the paste and pepper and stir to combine well. Cover the bowl with plastic wrap and refrigerate for 2–3 hours. Drain the fish well.

For the sauce, combine all the ingredients in a bowl and stir to combine well, until the sugar has dissolved.

Put the rice-stick noodles in a large bowl, cover with boiling water and stand for 5 minutes. Drain. Bring a large saucepan of water to the boil, add the noodles and cook for 2–3 minutes or until tender – or cook according to the packet instructions. Drain well.

Combine the rice flour, remaining turmeric and salt in a bowl. Add the fish and toss well to coat, shaking off any excess.

Heat 2 tablespoons of the oil in a large heavy-based frying pan over high heat. Add the spring onion and onion and cook, tossing often, for 4–5 minutes or until the onions are lightly charred. Add half the dill, toss for 1 minute or until the dill has wilted then transfer to a bowl.

Reduce the heat to medium and add the remaining oil to the pan. Add the fish, in a single layer, and cook, turning once, for 5–6 minutes or until the fish is cooked through. Scatter over the onion mixture and the remaining dill.

Divide the noodles among warmed bowls and divide the fish mixture over the noodles. Scatter over the peanuts and extra spring onion, and serve with the sauce on the side.

Fish with pork and ginger

· SERVES 4–6 AS PART OF A SHARED MEAL ·

This Cambodian-inspired dish may sound a bit odd – fish in a sauce made with pork, vinegar, sugar, fermented beans and dried mushrooms – but it works perfectly. As with most Cambodian fare, any spice-derived heat comes from adding fresh chilli yourself, so the chilli-shy are in safe territory here.

800 g (1 lb 12 oz) blue eye cod fillets or other firm, white-fleshed fish, skin on

cornflour (cornstarch) for dusting

1½ tablespoons vegetable oil

SAUCE

2 onions, halved and very thinly sliced

4 garlic cloves, very thinly sliced

1½ tablespoons vegetable oil

200 g (7 oz) pork loin or fillet, cut into thin strips

55 g (2 oz/¼ cup) very fine matchsticks of fresh ginger

2 tablespoons yellow bean sauce

1½ tablespoons caster (superfine) sugar

2 tablespoons clear rice vinegar

60 ml (2 fl oz/¼ cup) Chicken stock (see page 14)

4 dried shiitake mushrooms, soaked in boiling water for 30 minutes, drained and thinly sliced

TO SERVE

2 medium red chillies, trimmed and cut into very fine matchsticks, or to taste

1 spring onion (scallion), trimmed and thinly cut diagonally

coriander (cilantro) leaves

cooked fresh rice noodles

For the sauce, in a large frying pan over medium heat, cook the onion and garlic in the oil, stirring often, for 5–6 minutes or until light golden. Add the pork and ginger and cook for another 2–3 minutes or until the pork is nearly cooked and the ginger is fragrant. Add the soy bean sauce, sugar, rice vinegar, stock and mushrooms and bring to a simmer. Remove the pan from the heat, set aside and keep warm.

Dust the fish with the cornflour, shaking off any excess.

In a wok or large frying pan over medium–high heat, cook the fish, skin side down, in the oil for about 8 minutes, turning once, or until just cooked through. Add the reserved sauce and bring back to a simmer, shaking the wok gently so it heats evenly and to avoid breaking up the fish. Add a little water if the sauce is too thick.

Transfer the fish to serving plates or a large platter and spoon over the sauce. Scatter over the chillies, spring onion and coriander and serve immediately with the rice noodles.

Shaking beef

· SERVES 4 ·

This is another well-known and totally delicious dish from Vietnam, although it's also hugely popular in Cambodia, where it's often served with a fried egg and nearly always made using the peerless local spice, kampot pepper. In those countries, beef tends to be chewier than the meat we are used to, but we quite like using a really tender cut of beef (like sirloin or eye fillet) – or even venison – for this dish. It gets its name from the way you shake the pan or wok to cook the meat evenly.

750 g (1 lb 11 oz) beef or venison fillet, trimmed
    and cut into 3 cm (1¼ in) pieces
2 tablespoons clear rice vinegar
60 ml (2 fl oz/¼ cup) clear rice wine
2½ tablespoons lime juice
3 teaspoons caster (superfine) sugar
60 ml (2 fl oz/¼ cup) vegetable oil
2 red onions, halved and sliced
50 g (1¾ oz) butter, chopped
2 large bunches of watercress, sprigs picked, to serve
sesame seeds, to serve

MARINADE
4 garlic cloves, crushed
2 teaspoons freshly ground black pepper
2 teaspoons caster (superfine) sugar
2 tablespoons oyster sauce
1 tablespoon fish sauce
2 teaspoons light soy sauce
2 teaspoons dark soy sauce

For the marinade, combine all the ingredients in a large bowl and whisk to combine. Add the meat and toss to coat well. Cover the bowl with plastic wrap and refrigerate for 2–3 hours.

Put the meat in a colander over a bowl and drain well, reserving any marinade that drips through the colander.

Combine the rice vinegar, rice wine, lime juice and sugar in a bowl and set aside.

Heat half the oil in a wok over high heat. Add half the meat and half the red onion and cook, shaking the wok to keep the meat turning over, for about 4 minutes or until the meat is cooked through but still a little pink in the middle. Add half the butter and 1½ tablespoons of the rice vinegar mixture and shake the pan to combine well. Transfer the mixture to a bowl.

Add the remaining oil to the wok, then add the remaining red onion and meat and cook, shaking the wok, for 4 minutes or until the meat is just cooked through. Add the remaining butter and 1½ tablespoons more of the vinegar mixture and shake the pan to combine well.

Put the watercress on a serving platter, put the meat mixture on the top then drizzle over the juices from the wok, Sprinkle over the sesame seeds and serve immediately accompanied with any remaining vinegar mixture to add to taste.

Salt and pepper pork ribs

· **SERVES 4** ·

We love salt and pepper moistened with lemon (or lime) and used as a dip. This combination is excellent with marinated deep-fried quail, a common dish in Vietnam. So feel free to substitute six butterflied quail here for the ribs – deep-fry them until they are golden on the outside and still a tad pink and juicy in the middle. As avowed porkaholics (and ribaholics) we love this version, which is uber-easy to make. You can use either meaty short or long ribs here.

1.2 kg (2 lb 10 oz) pork short ribs, cut into approximately
   12 cm (4¾ in) lengths (ask your butcher to do this)
vegetable oil for deep-frying
250 g (9 oz/2 cups) cornflour (cornstarch), or as needed

MARINADE
1 teaspoon five-spice powder
2½ tablespoons shaoxing rice wine

1½ tablespoons dark soy sauce
2 tablespoons light soy sauce
1 tablespoon caster (superfine) sugar
5 garlic cloves, crushed

TO SERVE
salt flakes
crushed white peppercorns
lemon wedges

For the marinade, combine all the ingredients in a large bowl and stir to combine well until the sugar has dissolved. Add the ribs and, using clean hands, toss to combine, making sure the ribs are coated all over with the marinade. Cover the bowl tightly with plastic wrap and refrigerate for 3 hours or overnight, tossing the ribs occasionally.

Drain the ribs and discard any marinade.

Heat enough oil for deep-frying in a large saucepan until it reaches 170°C (340°F), or until a cube of bread turns golden in 20 seconds.

Toss half the ribs in the cornflour to coat well, shaking off any excess. Add the ribs to the pan and cook for 8 minutes or until the meat is tender and the ribs are crisp and golden on the outside. Transfer to a plate lined with paper towel to absorb any excess oil. Toss the remaining ribs in the cornflour then fry as above.

Put some salt flakes and a little white pepper in individual serving dishes and serve separately with lemon wedges for squeezing into the salt and pepper. Dip the ribs into this mixture before eating.

Tamarind prawns

· SERVES 4–6 AS PART OF A SHARED MEAL ·

Thick, sour, sweet and delicious all at the same time, we reckon this punchy sauce is about the best thing to ever happen to a wok-tossed prawn. Prawns are customarily fried or grilled unpeeled in Southeast Asia – diners there love nothing more than sucking out the head juices and chewing on crisp shells. We always envy the huge ones you can get in Asia and for this dish, the bigger the prawns, the better. The actual variety you use – tiger, king or banana – doesn't matter too much.

2½ tablespoons tamarind pulp
250 ml (8½ fl oz/1 cup) boiling water
60 ml (2 fl oz/¼ cup) kecap manis
8 garlic cloves, crushed
1 tablespoon shaved palm sugar (jaggery)
1 teaspoon freshly ground black pepper
1 kg (2 lb 3 oz) large raw tiger prawns (shrimp)
2½ tablespoons vegetable oil

COCONUT AND GREEN CHILLI SAMBAL
100 g (3½ oz/1 cup) fresh grated or thawed frozen grated coconut (see page 28)
3 medium green chillies, chopped
3 red Asian shallots, chopped
2 tablespoons lime juice
handful of coriander (cilantro) leaves, chopped

Combine the tamarind pulp with the boiling water in a bowl and stand for 20 minutes. Strain the mixture through a sieve, using your fingers to press down on the solids to extract as much liquid as possible. Discard the solids. Combine in a large bowl with the kecap manis, garlic, sugar and pepper and stir to mix well.

Using kitchen scissors, trim the legs and feelers off the prawns. Cut through the shell along the back of each prawn and remove the digestive tract – do not peel the prawns. Add the prawns to the tamarind mixture and, using your hands, rub the mixture all over the prawns well so it goes into the cut in the shells. Cover the bowl with plastic wrap and refrigerate for 2 hours.

Bring to room temperature and remove the prawns from the tamarind mixture, reserving the marinade.

For the coconut and green chilli sambal, combine all the ingredients in a food processor. Using the pulse button, process until a coarse paste forms. Season to taste with salt and freshly ground black pepper. Set aside.

Heat the oil in a wok over high heat until nearly smoking. Add the prawns and stir-fry for about 6 minutes or until nearly cooked through. Add the reserved marinade and continue to cook, stirring, until the mixture is very reduced, and the prawns are well coated and cooked through. Serve with the sambal.

Crisp mussel pancakes

· **SERVES 4** ·

This is quintessential all-day Thai street food, known as *hoy tod*. The key here is to get this pancake crisp, so choose the right heavy-based pan and watch your heat! Smaller mussels are better, if you can source them, otherwise cut them in half if they are a larger variety. It's best to cook these pancakes in batches.

1 kg (2 lb 3 oz) mussels, scrubbed and debearded
130 g (4½ oz/1 cup) tapioca flour
90 g (3 oz/½ cup) rice flour
½ teaspoon salt
80 ml (2½ fl oz/⅓ cup) vegetable oil, or as necessary
4 spring onions (scallions), trimmed and thinly sliced
4 eggs, lightly beaten

200 g (7 oz) bean sprouts
4 garlic cloves, finely chopped
2 tablespoons fish sauce

TO SERVE
Sweet chilli sauce (see page 15) or Sriracha sauce
handful of coriander (cilantro) leaves

Put the mussels in a saucepan over high heat with 250 ml (8½ fl oz/1 cup) water and cover the pan tightly. Cook, shaking the pan often, for 4–5 minutes or until the mussels open. Remove the pan from the heat and drain the mussels well. When cool enough to handle, remove the mussel meat from the shells, discarding the shells.

Combine the flours, salt and 250 ml (8½ fl oz/1 cup) water in a bowl and whisk until a smooth batter forms. Add a little extra water if necessary – it should have the consistency of pouring (single/light) cream.

Heat a large, heavy-based frying pan over medium–high heat. Add a tablespoon of the oil and heat until it starts to smoke. Add about 60 ml (2 fl oz/¼ cup) of the batter, working quickly to swirl the pan so it coats the base evenly. Scatter a quarter of the mussels and spring onions over and cook for about 2 minutes or until the edges are golden and crisp. Fold over in half and cook for another minute. Using a large, flat-bladed

knife or sharp spatula, cut the pancake into 3 pieces and turn each piece over. Pour a quarter of the beaten egg over and around the pancake pieces and cook for 1 minute or until the eggs set on the base and start to turn golden. Turn the pancake pieces over and cook for another minute or until the other side is golden and the egg is set. Transfer to a plate.

Add a little extra oil to the frying pan, if necessary. Add a quarter of the bean sprouts, a quarter of the garlic and 2 teaspoons of the fish sauce to the pan and stir-fry for 1 minute. Pour over the pancake. Repeat with the remaining batter, eggs and other ingredients to make 4 pancakes.

Cut the pancakes in half, if desired, before serving with the sweet chilli sauce and garnished with the coriander.

Fried spiced fish

· SERVES 6 AS PART OF A SHARED MEAL ·

Salmon is not exactly an Asian fish, but we really love it and find its sweet oiliness stands up well to most flavourings. If you wish to simplify things here, or just don't fancy the chew of raw lemongrass, leave the sambal out – although its fresh, fragrant presence does add a lovely dimension to this stunning dish.

4 x 200 g (7 oz) salmon or ocean trout fillets, skin removed
60 ml (2 fl oz/¼ cup) vegetable oil
Lemongrass sambal (see page 18) to serve

SPICE PASTE
1 tomato
1½ teaspoons trasi (Indonesian shrimp paste)
3 teaspoons tamarind pulp
60 ml (2 fl oz/¼ cup) boiling water

10 candlenuts, chopped
3 lemongrass stems, white part only, chopped
8 medium red chillies, chopped
5 cm (2 in) piece fresh ginger, chopped
8 garlic cloves, chopped
1½ teaspoons ground turmeric
1 tablespoon ground coriander
80 ml (2½ fl oz/⅓ cup) vegetable oil

For the spice paste, bring a saucepan of water to the boil. Use a small sharp knife to remove the core end of the tomato and cut a small cross shape in the base. Plunge the tomato into the pan of boiling water for 30 seconds then transfer to a bowl of iced water. Drain well then peel the tomato, chop and set aside.

Wrap the trasi in foil. Heat a small, heavy-based frying pan over medium heat, add the wrapped trasi then dry-fry for 2 minutes on each side, or until fragrant. Cool and unwrap.

Combine the tamarind pulp with the boiling water in a bowl and stand for 20 minutes. Strain the mixture through a sieve, using your fingers to press down on the solids to extract as much liquid as possible. Discard the solids.

In a food processor, combine the candlenuts, lemongrass, chillies, ginger, garlic, turmeric, coriander, trasi and oil and process until a smooth paste forms. Add the tomato and tamarind liquid and process until well combined.

Using tweezers, remove the pin bones from the salmon and cut each piece in half crossways.

Combine the fish and spice paste in a bowl, turning to coat the fish well. Cover the bowl with plastic wrap and refrigerate, for 1 hour.

Heat a heavy-based, non-stick frying pan over medium heat, add the oil and swirl to coat the base of the pan. Add the fish, making sure it is still well coated in the spice paste, and cook for 4 minutes or until half cooked. Turn the fish and cook for another 4 minutes or until cooked through but still a little pink in the middle. Transfer the fish to a plate and cool slightly.

When cool enough to handle, use your hands to break the fish into coarse pieces and place on a serving platter. Scatter the lemongrass sambal over and serve.

Rice & Noodles

The backbone of Southeast Asian cuisines, rice and noodles play a far wider role than simply mere carb-fillers. They show up in a range of dishes across the whole gamut of Southeast Asian cooking – in salads, gutsy soups, stir-fries, clay-pot casseroles and plenty more besides. We can't decide which we like more – the satisfying chew of sticky rice in Vietnamese *xoi*, the slippery familiarity of rice-stick noodles in classic *pad Thai*, or the resilient bounce of fresh egg noodles swimming in a bowl of steaming *mee rebus* gravy. We love them all.

Fried hokkien mee

· SERVES 4 ·

This common street-food dish has its origins in the Fujian province of China, and you will find a few versions around Malaysia. The version here is closer to the Kuala Lumpur approach of *hokkien char mee,* which uses dark soy sauce in the dish. It's easy to prepare, and a good, large wok certainly helps as you do need to generate plenty of heat. The pineapple and cucumber sambal adds freshness and crunch.

500 g (1 lb 2 oz) squid, cleaned, tentacles reserved

600 g (1 lb 5 oz) fresh (hokkien) egg noodles

boiling water

80 ml (2½ fl oz/⅓ cup) peanut oil

3 eggs, beaten well

500 g (1 lb 2 oz) raw king prawns (shrimp), shelled, deveined and tails left intact

3 garlic cloves, crushed

200 g (7 oz) barbecued Chinese pork (char siu) (available from Asian barbecue shops), thinly sliced

200 g (7 oz) bean sprouts

250 ml (8½ fl oz/1 cup) Chicken stock (see page 14)

1 tablespoon dark soy sauce

1 tablespoon light soy sauce

Pineapple and cucumber sambal (see page 19) to serve

Using a sharp knife, cut down one side of each fresh squid tube to open them out flat. Score the inside surface of the squid bodies in a criss-cross pattern, then cut into 2.5 cm (1 in) pieces and reserve. Chop the tentacles.

Put the noodles in a large bowl and pour boiling water over to cover. Stand for 1 minute or until they have softened, then drain well.

Heat 1 tablespoon of the oil in a wok over medium–high heat, swirling to coat the wok. Pour in the eggs, again swirling to coat the wok, this time to form a thin omelette, then cook for 1–2 minutes or until set. Turn out onto a chopping board and thinly slice the omelette. Set aside.

Add half the remaining oil to the wok. Increase the heat to high, add the prawns and stir-fry for 2–3 minutes or until just cooked through. Transfer to a plate.

In the wok, stir-fry the squid and garlic in the remaining oil for 2 minutes or until the squid is nearly tender. Add the pork and bean sprouts, return the prawns to the wok and toss to combine well. Add the noodles, stock, soy sauces and sliced omelette and cook for another 2 minutes or until the liquid is slightly reduced and everything is heated through.

Serve with the pineapple and cucumber sambal.

See image on pages 188–189

Fried rice cake

· SERVES 4 ·

Char koay kak originally comes from southern China, and versions are consumed all over Malaysia and Singapore. We've opted for the Penang version, but there's also a popular style that uses preserved daikon (white radish). This is hawker food at its finest, using rice and tapioca flour, which is cooked and cut into squares. This dish is usually eaten for breakfast or supper, but we believe you should eat it anytime. It's that good.

80 ml (2½ fl oz/⅓ cup) vegetable oil, plus extra
  if necessary
3 eggs, well beaten
3 garlic cloves, crushed
2 tablespoons preserved radish (available from Asian
  supermarkets), rinsed
2–3 tablespoons chilli paste
60 ml (2 fl oz/¼ cup) light soy sauce
1½ tablespoons dark soy sauce

200 g (7 oz) bean sprouts
½ bunch of garlic chives, cut into 3 cm
  (1¼ in) pieces

RICE CAKE
300 g (10½ oz) rice flour
80 g (2¾ oz) tapioca flour
1 teaspoon salt

For the rice cake, oil the sides and base of a 24 cm (9½ in) square baking dish. Combine all the ingredients in a large bowl and stir to combine well. Stirring constantly, add 1 litre (34 fl oz/ 4 cups) water and mix until smooth.

Heat a wok over medium–low heat, add the mixture and cook, stirring constantly to prevent lumps forming, for about 4 minutes or until thickened. Pour into the prepared dish, using a wet spatula to smooth the surface.

Steam the mixture in a wok or steamer for 20 minutes, or until firm. Remove from the heat and cool to room temperature.

Turn the steamed cake out onto a chopping board then cut it into 1 cm (½ in) squares.

Heat 2 tablespoons of the oil in a large wok over medium–high heat. Add half the rice cake pieces and stir-fry, taking care not to break up the cubes, for about 15 minutes or until deep golden and crisp on the outside. Using a slotted spoon, transfer to a plate lined with paper towel. Cook the remaining cubes, adding more vegetable oil as necessary.

Add the eggs to the wok and, cook, stirring constantly, for 3–4 minutes or until the eggs are firm and scrambled. Transfer to a bowl. Add 1 tablespoon of the oil to the wok, add the garlic and cook for 1 minute or until fragrant. Add the preserved radish, rice cake cubes, chilli paste, soy sauces, bean sprouts and egg and stir-fry for 4–5 minutes or until heated through. Transfer to plates, scatter over the garlic chives and serve hot.

Yellow chicken rice

· SERVES 4 ·

This dish is Thailand's answer to biryani. The local name is *khao mok gai,* meaning rice with chicken. It's very popular among the Muslim–Thai population and has Indian/Persian influences. The rice is cooked along with the chicken and spices to produce a beautifully aromatic one-pot dish.

4 chicken leg quarters
2 teaspoons freshly ground black pepper
1 tablespoon Malaysian curry powder
2 teaspoons ground turmeric
2 teaspoons ground cumin
2 teaspoons ground coriander
1 teaspoon chilli powder
125 g (4 oz/½ cup) Greek-style yoghurt
60 ml (2 fl oz/¼ cup) vegetable oil
1 small onion, halved and very thinly sliced
4 garlic cloves, crushed
400 g (14 oz/2 cups) jasmine rice, rinsed
375 ml (12½ fl oz/1½ cups) boiling water
200 ml (7 fl oz) coconut milk
1 cinnamon stick
6 cardamom pods, crushed

SAUCE
80 ml (2½ fl oz/⅓ cup) clear rice vinegar
1½ tablespoons caster (superfine) sugar
1 teaspoon salt
2 medium green chillies, finely chopped
2 spring onions (scallions), trimmed and
  very finely chopped
1½ tablespoons finely chopped fresh ginger
large handful of coriander (cilantro), finely chopped

TO SERVE
Fried shallots (see page 26)
sliced cucumber and tomato (optional)

Using a large, sharp knife, cut through the middle joint of each chicken leg quarter to separate the thigh from the drumstick. Trim the excess backbone from the thighs and cut each thigh in half through the middle thigh bone.

Combine the pepper, curry powder, turmeric, cumin, coriander and chilli powder in a bowl. Transfer half this mixture and the yoghurt to a large bowl, reserving the remaining spice mixture. Add the chicken to the bowl and, using your hands, rub the mixture all over the chicken. Cover the bowl with plastic wrap and refrigerate for 4 hours or overnight.

Wipe any excess marinade off the chicken and discard the marinade.

Preheat the oven to 180°C (350°F). Heat half the vegetable oil in a large ovenproof casserole over medium heat. Add the chicken and cook, turning often, for 6 minutes or until deep golden.

Transfer to a plate. Add the remaining oil to the casserole, add the onion and garlic and cook, stirring, for 2–3 minutes or until starting to soften. Add the reserved spice mixture and cook, stirring, for another minute or until fragrant. Add the rice and stir to coat well. Add the boiling water, coconut milk, cinnamon stick and cardamom pods. Put the chicken on top of the rice, cover the casserole with a tight-fitting lid and transfer to the oven. Cook for 25 minutes or until the chicken is cooked through and the rice is tender.

For the sauce, combine the rice vinegar, sugar and salt with 1½ tablespoons water and stir to combine. Add the remaining ingredients and stir to combine.

Serve the chicken and rice with the fried shallots and sliced cucumber and tomato, if using, and the sauce on the side.

Claypot noodles and prawns

· SERVES 2–3, OR 4 AS PART OF A SHARED MEAL ·

Cellophane, or bean-thread, noodles are mostly associated with Chinese cuisine, but the Thais also have a few nifty uses for them, notably in this easy one-pot dish–although the noodles have no appreciable flavour of their own. However, what these noodles do offer is great texture plus the ability to absorb and transmit other flavours really, really well. Instead of prawns, you can use cleaned raw blue-swimmer crabs or other medium-sized crabs, cut into pieces.

200 g (7 oz) cellophane (bean-thread) noodles

500 g (1 lb 2 oz) jumbo raw tiger or king prawns (shrimp) (about 8)

1 teaspoon ground white pepper

1 tablespoon oyster sauce

1 tablespoon shaoxing rice wine

1 tablespoon light soy sauce

3 teaspoons dark soy sauce

2 teaspoons caster (superfine) sugar

large pinch of five-spice powder

2 Chinese sausages (lap cheong), thinly sliced

1½ tablespoons finely chopped fresh ginger

5–6 Chinese celery stalks, chopped, leaves reserved and chopped

4 garlic cloves, chopped

6 large red Asian shallots, thinly sliced

1 tablespoon vegetable oil

handful of coriander (cilantro) leaves, chopped

4 spring onions (scallions), trimmed and thinly sliced

200 ml (7 fl oz) Chicken stock (see page 14)

Seafood nam jim (see page 16) for dipping

Put the noodles in a large bowl and add enough hot water to cover. Soak for 15 minutes then drain well. Cut the noodles into 5 cm (2 in) lengths with kitchen scissors and set aside.

Meanwhile, using kitchen scissors, cut through each prawn shell along the back, from behind the head to the tail, and remove the digestive tract. Leave the shells on but use scissors to trim the legs and feelers. Set aside.

Combine the pepper, oyster sauce, rice wine, soy sauces, sugar and five-spice powder in a bowl. Toss through the noodles and set aside.

In a large claypot over medium heat, cook the sausages, ginger, celery stalks, garlic and shallots in the oil, stirring, for about 5 minutes or until the shallots are light golden. Add the coriander and spring onion and cook, stirring, for 3 minutes or until the vegetables have softened slightly. Put the prawns over the mixture in an even layer then add the noodle mixture in an even layer. Add the stock, cover the pot with a lid and cook for 10–15 minutes or until the prawns are just cooked through. Spoon the cooking liquid over the noodles, adding a little extra stock or water if necessary – the mixture should not be wet.

Transfer to a serving dish, scatter over the reserved celery leaves and serve with the seafood nam jim for dipping.

Rice noodles with tofu and jicama

· **SERVES 4** ·

Slippery, cool rice noodles, crunchy and sweet jicama, aromatic herbs and slightly pungent *nuoc cham* provide a fabulous bowlful of contrasting tastes and textures – the whole thing finished off smoothly with a slick of hot, creamy coconut milk. Heaven in a bowl! Jicama is also known as yam bean and is used in Mexican and Chinese cooking as well as in Vietnamese – the culinary inspiration here – so try your local Asian or Latin supermarket. With its crisper-than-crisp, super-light texture, jicama is a little difficult to replace but, if you're really struggling, substitute raw carrot.

400 g (14 oz) dried wide rice noodles

200 g (7 oz) mung bean sprouts

250 g (9 oz) jicama (about 1 medium), peeled and cut into fine matchsticks

2 Lebanese (short) cucumbers, cut into fine matchsticks

2 spring onions (scallions), trimmed and cut into fine matchsticks

250 g (9 oz) fried tofu (available from Asian supermarkets), cut into thin batons

100 g (3½ oz) roasted unsalted peanuts, coarsely chopped

handful of coriander (cilantro)

handful of Thai basil, torn

handful of perilla leaves, torn

220 g (8 oz/1 cup) Pickled carrot (see page 26), drained

Nuoc cham (see page 16)

400 ml (13½ fl oz) thick coconut milk, heated

Cook the rice noodles according to the packet instructions. Drain and cool under running water, then drain again.

Place the noodles, mung bean sprouts, vegetables, tofu, peanuts, herbs, pickled carrots and 125 ml (4 fl oz/½ cup) of the nuoc cham in a large bowl. Toss to combine well, then divide among serving bowls.

Serve immediately with the remaining nuoc cham and the hot coconut milk to pour over to taste.

Pad Thai

· SERVES 2 ·

Arguably the best known exponent of this famous dish is Pad Thai Thip Samai, located on Thanon Mahachai in the old part of Bangkok. They start serving at 5 am, working from huge woks fired over blazingly hot charcoal, which can accommodate around a dozen portions at a time. They cook a few versions, the most elegant is called *pad thai haw kai goong sot*, and it comes enclosed in the finest of egg omelettes and topped with coriander. You can easily double this version to serve four, but it's best to cook two portions at a time, so as not to overcrowd your wok. If you like, add some shelled and deveined prawns, firm tofu and sliced, boneless, skinless chicken breast or pork fillet.

2 tablespoons dried shrimp, soaked in warm water for 30 minutes, drained

2 tablespoons shaved palm sugar (jaggery)

2½ tablespoons lime juice or lemon juice

2 tablespoons fish sauce

2 garlic cloves, finely chopped

60 ml (2 fl oz/¼ cup) peanut oil

3 spring onions (scallions), thinly sliced

2 large eggs, lightly beaten

150 g (5½ oz) dried rice-stick noodles, soaked in hot water for 8 minutes or according to the packet instructions, drained

1½ tablespoons Chinese pickled radish (available from Asian supermarkets), finely chopped

2½ tablespoons finely chopped unsalted roasted peanuts

65 g (2¼ oz) mung bean sprouts, trimmed

TO SERVE

chopped unsalted roasted peanuts

chopped trimmed mung bean sprouts

chilli powder or flakes

coriander (cilantro) sprigs

lime cheeks

Finely grind the dried shrimp in an electric spice grinder. Alternatively, use a mortar and pestle.

Combine the palm sugar, lime juice, fish sauce and 1 tablespoon water in a bowl, stirring until the sugar has dissolved.

In a wok over medium heat, cook the garlic in the oil, stirring, for 1 minute or until fragrant. Add the spring onion and eggs and cook, stirring, for about 2 minutes or until the eggs are starting to set. Add the drained noodles, stirring to break them up and incorporate the eggs. Add the fish sauce mixture and

cook, tossing the wok often, for about 3 minutes or until the liquid is mostly absorbed. Add the dried shrimp powder, pickled radish, peanuts and bean sprouts and toss to combine well. Stir-fry for 1–2 minutes or until the mixture is quite dry and the sprouts are wilted slightly. Taste for seasoning – it should be slightly sweet, salty and sour. Add more sugar, lime juice and fish sauce to taste.

Divide the pad Thai among serving plates and top with the peanuts, sprouts, some chilli powder and coriander. Serve immediately with lime cheeks on the side.

Rice noodle salad

· **SERVES 6** ·

This vibrant, zesty salad from Malaysia is known locally as *kerabu bee hoon*, which loosely means spicy, sweet and sour salad with rice vermicelli – at least, that's our interpretation! The dish is eaten throughout the day from breakfast to dinner, as well as being a go-to snack in between. It epitomises the beautiful flavours of Southeast Asia – lemongrass, kaffir lime leaves, garlic, coconut and chilli – all easily slapped together with rice vermicelli to soak up all the goodness.

80 g (2¾ oz/⅓ cup) dried shrimp

1½ tablespoons very finely chopped fresh galangal

50 g (1¾ oz/½ cup) fresh grated or thawed frozen grated coconut (see page 28)

200 g (7 oz) dried rice vermicelli

500 g (1 lb 2 oz) cooked medium king or tiger prawns (shrimp), shelled, deveined and tails left intact

6 red Asian shallots, very thinly sliced or ½ red onion, very thinly sliced

large handful of mint leaves, torn, to serve

coriander (cilantro) leaves to serve

DRESSING

1 tablespoon belacan (Malaysian shrimp paste)

5 red bird's eye chillies, chopped

6 medium red chillies, chopped

2 garlic cloves, chopped

100 ml (3½ fl oz) lime juice

1½ tablespoons caster (superfine) sugar

2 tablespoons light soy sauce

For the dressing, wrap the belacan in foil. Heat a small, heavy-based frying pan over medium heat, add the wrapped belacan then dry-fry for 2 minutes on each side, or until fragrant. Cool and unwrap. Transfer to a food processor with the chillies and garlic and process until a smooth paste forms. Alternatively, use a mortar and pestle. Combine in a small bowl with the remaining dressing ingredients and 2 tablespoons water and stir to combine well until the sugar has dissolved.

Finely grind the dried shrimp in an electric spice grinder until a coarse powder forms – process in batches if necessary. Transfer to a frying pan over medium–low heat, add the galangal and coconut and dry-fry for 5–6 minutes or until fragrant and the coconut is light golden.

Put the rice vermicelli in a bowl, pour over cold water to cover then stand for 15 minutes or until softened. Drain well. Cook the noodles in boiling water for 2 minutes or until softened, or cook according to the packet instructions.

In a large bowl combine the prawns with the coconut mixture, noodles, shallots and the dressing and toss to mix well. Transfer to bowls or plates, scatter over the mint and coriander and serve.

Green nasi goreng

· SERVES 4 ·

If there's one Indonesian dish most people know, it's nasi goreng. When translated as 'fried rice' it sounds rather prosaic, but when cooked well, this is a dish that's anything but ordinary. In Java it's a much-loved breakfast dish. Our version emphasises green vegetables – and lots of them – making it nutritious as well as completely delicious.

8 medium raw king prawns (shrimp)

90 ml (3 fl oz) vegetable oil

4 wing beans, halved lengthways, thinly sliced

1 bunch of snake (yard-long) beans, trimmed and very thinly sliced

300 g (10½ oz) Chinese cabbage (wombok), very finely chopped

2 boneless, skinless chicken breasts, cut into 2 cm (¾ in) pieces

375 g (13 oz/3 cups) cold, cooked long-grain rice

2½ tablespoons kecap manis

1 tablespoon light soy sauce

6 kaffir lime leaves, central vein removed, very thinly sliced

1 Lebanese (short) cucumber, halved lengthways, seeded and cut into 2 cm (¾ in) pieces

3 spring onions (scallions), trimmed and very thinly sliced

large handful of coriander (cilantro), chopped

large handful of Thai basil, chopped

4 eggs

PASTE

8 long green chillies, chopped

4 green bird's eye chillies, chopped

1 teaspoon trasi (Indonesian shrimp paste)

6 garlic cloves

6 red Asian shallots, chopped

TO SERVE

Fried shallots (see page 26)

fried prawn crackers

chilli sauce

kecap mani

For the paste, combine all the ingredients in a food processor and process until a smooth paste forms. Alternatively, use a mortar and pestle.

Using kitchen scissors, cut through the shell of each prawn along the back, from behind the head to the tail, and remove the digestive tract. Trim the legs and feelers. Set the prawns aside.

Heat 2 tablespoons of the oil in a wok over high heat, add the wing beans, snake beans and cabbage and stir-fry for 5–6 minutes or until the vegetables have softened. Transfer to a bowl.

Wipe out the wok. Add another tablespoon of oil to the wok, add the paste and chicken and cook, stirring constantly, for 8 minutes or until the chicken is nearly cooked through. Add the rice, kecap manis, soy sauce, cooked vegetables and lime leaves to the wok and stir-fry for 10–12 minutes until well combined and the rice is heated through. Add the cucumber, spring onion, coriander and basil and toss to combine well.

Meanwhile, heat a chargrill pan over medium–high heat and brush the prawns with a little of the remaining oil. Grill the prawns for 2–3 minutes on each side or until cooked through. Set aside and keep warm.

Heat the remaining oil in a large frying pan over a medium heat. Carefully crack the eggs into the pan and fry for 2–3 minutes or until the edges start to crisp. Turn the eggs over and continue to cook for another 30 seconds.

Divide the rice among warmed serving bowls, top each with 2 prawns, a fried egg and some fried shallots. Serve the prawn crackers on the side with the chilli sauce and kecap manis.

Nasi lemak

· SERVES 4 ·

Nasi lemak means 'coconut rice', and anyone who has ever ventured to Singapore or Malaysia will have encountered this sensational dish. There, it's pure street food, served with all the essential accompaniments – deep-fried peanuts, boiled egg, a sambal made of ikan bilis (dried anchovies), sliced cucumber, maybe some grilled fish and a few spoonfuls of curry. It often comes wrapped as a parcel inside fragrant banana leaves, or served on a plate lined with a banana leaf. It's an all-round dish, popular for breakfast, but it's also consumed throughout the day and into the night. It's one of our all-time favourites.

400 g (14 oz/2 cups) long-grain white rice, rinsed and drained
375 ml (12½ fl oz/1½ cups) coconut milk
2 pandan leaves, bruised and each tied in a knot
4 mackerel fillets
vegetable oil for brushing
4 hard-boiled eggs, halved

TO SERVE
4 pieces of banana leaf
160 g (5½ oz/1 cup) roasted unsalted peanuts (optional)
1 telegraph (long) cucumber, peeled and sliced
Sambal ikan bilis (see page 20)
Fried shallots (see page 26)

Combine the rice, coconut milk, pandan leaves and 310 ml (10½ fl oz/1¼ cups) water in a saucepan and bring to a simmer. Cover with a tight-fitting lid and cook for 15 minutes or until the liquid is absorbed. Remove from the heat and stand, covered, for 10 minutes or until the rice is tender.

While the rice is resting, brush the mackerel with oil and heat a chargrill pan or barbecue to medium–high. Cook, turning once, for 5–6 minutes or until the fish is cooked through.

Line four serving plates with a piece of banana leaf. Place a spoonful of rice in the middle of each then place the egg, mackerel, peanuts, if using, cucumber and sambal around the rice and serve.

Shrimp paste fried rice with pork

· SERVES 4–6 ·

This incredible Thai dish really does have it all going on in the flavour department – hot, sour, spicy, sweet and pungent. The shrimp paste flavour in the rice is strong, but it's tempered by all the various accompaniments, among them the most delicious, sweet and sticky pork.

500 g (1 lb 2 oz/2½ cups) jasmine rice, rinsed

120 g (4½ oz/1 cup) dried shrimp, soaked in warm water for 30 minutes, drained well

60 ml (2 fl oz/¼ cup) vegetable oil

3 eggs, well beaten

2½ tablespoons gapi (Thai shrimp paste)

1 tablespoon caster (superfine) sugar

SWEET PORK

600 g (1 lb 5 oz) pork neck, cut into 1.5 cm (½ in) pieces

6 garlic cloves, crushed

6 coriander (cilantro) roots, scrubbed and finely chopped

4 red Asian shallots, finely chopped

1½ tablespoons vegetable oil

75 g (2¾ oz) shaved palm sugar (jaggery)

2½ tablespoons fish sauce

1½ tablespoons light soy sauce

3 teaspoons dark soy sauce

TO SERVE

1 large green mango, peeled and cut into fine matchsticks

1 large Lebanese (short) cucumber, cut into fine matchsticks

6 red Asian shallots, thinly sliced

2 limes, cut into halves or wedges

6 medium red chillies, thinly sliced

handful of coriander (cilantro) sprigs

For the sweet pork, in a wok over medium–high heat, cook the pork, garlic, coriander and shallots in the oil, stirring, for 3–4 minutes or until the pork has changed colour. Add the remaining ingredients and bring to the boil. Reduce the heat to medium and cook for 20 minutes or until the pork is tender and the liquid has reduced to form a very thick glaze.

Combine the rice and 750 ml (25½ fl oz/3 cups) water in a saucepan over medium–high heat. Cover with a tight-fitting lid and bring to a simmer. Cook for 12–14 minutes or until all the water has been absorbed – try not to lift the lid too often or too much steam will escape. Remove the pan from the heat and stand for 10 minutes, then spread over the base of a baking dish to cool.

In a wok over medium heat, cook the dried shrimp in the oil for 2–3 minutes until crisp. Transfer to paper towel to drain. Remove all but 1½ tablespoons of the oil from the wok, reserving the oil. Increase the heat to medium–high and add the egg to the wok, swirling to thinly coat the base. Cook for 3 minutes, swirling, or until the egg is just set.

Turn the cooked egg onto a chopping board. When cool enough to handle, roll the omelette up and cut into very thin slices.

Return the reserved oil to the wok and reduce the heat to medium. Add the gapi and cook for 1 minute or until fragrant. Add the sugar and rice and cook, tossing often to mix well, for 4 minutes or until the rice is heated through and combined well.

Place the rice on a large serving plate and top with slices of omelette. Serve the fried dried shrimp, sweet pork and the remaining ingredients in separate bowls, for the diners to mix as they desire.

Sticky rice with chicken

· **SERVES 4–6** ·

This Vietnamese dish is called *xoi man*. *Xoi* is a popular sticky rice–based breakfast dish found all over the country, and there are many variations. Some are flavoured with peanuts, some with green beans and other types with bitter melon or black beans. We love this Ho Chi Minh City version, which is very quick to prepare and cook, providing you've first soaked your sticky rice overnight. You can have this on the table within 20 minutes, with minimal washing up afterwards – it's a winner all round. We love it for dinner.

600 g (1 lb 5 oz/3 cups) sticky (glutinous) white rice, soaked overnight in water to cover, drained well

3 garlic cloves, crushed

4 large red Asian shallots, thinly sliced

5 x 160 g (5½ oz) Chinese sausages (lap cheong) (available from Asian supermarkets), thinly sliced

600 g (1 lb 5 oz) boneless, skinless chicken thighs, trimmed and cut into 2.5 cm (1 in) pieces

2 tablespoons vegetable oil

30 g (1 oz/¼ cup) dried shrimp, soaked in warm water for 30 minutes, drained

2 tablespoons light soy sauce

1 tablespoon fish sauce

3 teaspoons caster (superfine) sugar

2 spring onions (scallions), thinly sliced

TO SERVE

coriander (cilantro)

pork floss (available from Asian supermarkets)

Fried shallots (see page 26)

Nuoc cham (see page 16)

Place the rice in a steamer lined with muslin (cheesecloth) or a clean tea (dish) towel. Cover the steamer and cook for 20 minutes or until the rice is tender. Set aside.

In a large wok over medium heat, cook the garlic, shallots, sausage and chicken in the oil, stirring often, for about 7 minutes or until the chicken is nearly cooked through. Add the drained shrimp and cook, tossing the wok, for another 2–3 minutes or until the shrimp are slightly softened. Add the remaining ingredients and toss to mix well. Add the rice to the wok and use a wooden spoon to break it up gently and distribute it through the other ingredients. Cook, stirring, for 2–3 minutes to heat the rice through.

Transfer to a serving bowl or platter and top with the coriander, pork floss and fried shallots. Serve with the nuoc cham on the side.

Mee rebus

· **SERVES 6** ·

Mee rebus translates as 'boiled noodles', and is a popular dish in Singapore and Malaysia. With its complex sauce based on sweet potato, it's a gutsy dish, and is sometimes made with beef. The beauty of it is all the myriad accompaniments – tofu, hard-boiled eggs and chilli. There are no set rules here; just put the lot in the middle of the table and get your family or guests to help themselves.

800 g (1 lb 12 oz) (about 2 medium) orange sweet potatoes, peeled and chopped
2 tablespoons vegetable oil
1.5 litres (51 fl oz/6 cups) Chicken stock (see page 14)
80 ml (2½ fl oz/⅓ cup) yellow bean sauce
2 tablespoons light soy sauce
125 ml (4 fl oz/½ cup) coconut milk
60 g (2 oz/⅓ cup) shaved palm sugar (jaggery)
2 tablespoons potato starch
400 g (14 oz) bean sprouts
840 g (1 lb 14 oz) fresh thin yellow egg noodles

PASTE

2½ tablespoons dried shrimp
8–10 large dried red chillies, soaked in boiling water for 30 minutes, drained
6 garlic cloves, chopped

4 red Asian shallots, chopped
2 lemongrass stems, white part only, chopped
5 cm (2 in) piece fresh galangal, chopped
8 candlenuts
2 teaspoons Malaysian curry powder

TO SERVE

10 fried tofu puffs, sliced (available from Asian supermarkets)
6 hard-boiled eggs, halved
2–3 red bird's eye chillies, thinly sliced
Chilli sambal (see page 18)

For the paste, finely grind the dried shrimp in an electric spice grinder. Transfer to a food processor with the remaining paste ingredients and process until smooth. Alternatively, use a mortar and pestle.

Meanwhile, cook the sweet potatoes in boiling water for about 12 minutes or until tender. Drain well. Transfer to a food processor or blender and process until smooth.

In a large saucepan over medium heat, cook the paste in the oil, stirring, for 3 minutes or until fragrant. Stir in the sweet potato, stock, soy bean sauce, soy sauce, coconut milk and palm sugar and bring to a simmer. Cover and cook over low heat for 10 minutes, stirring occasionally. Season to taste with salt and freshly ground black pepper.

Combine the potato starch with 60 ml (2 fl oz/¼ cup) water to make a smooth paste. Stirring constantly, add it to the sauce and cook, stirring, until it simmers and thickens.

Bring a large saucepan of water to the boil. Add the bean sprouts and cook for 1 minute or until softened. Transfer to a bowl using a slotted spoon.

Return the water in the saucepan to the boil, add the noodles and cook for 3 minutes, or according to the packet instructions, until tender. Drain well.

Divide the noodles among large bowls and ladle the sauce over. Divide the sprouts, tofu puffs and eggs among the bowls, scatter over the red chillies and serve with the chilli sambal on the side.

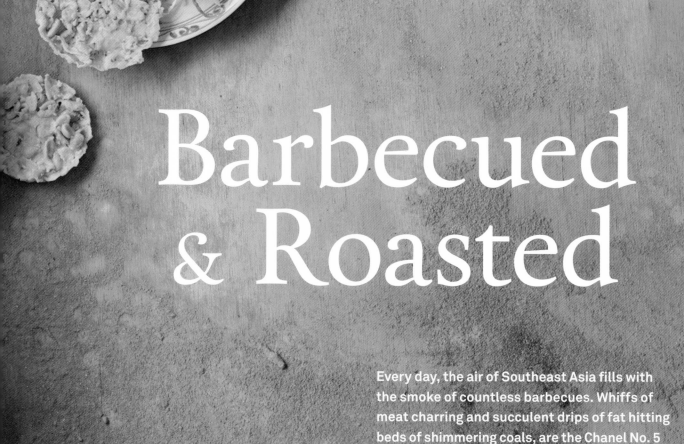

Barbecued & Roasted

Every day, the air of Southeast Asia fills with the smoke of countless barbecues. Whiffs of meat charring and succulent drips of fat hitting beds of shimmering coals, are the Chanel No. 5 of food fragrances to us. From whole calves spit-roasted in Cambodia and barbecued goat devoured in Laos, to the juicy discs of porky mince for *bun cha*, charred in the back streets of Hanoi, it's fair to say we've eaten our body weight in Asian barbecue. It never tastes quite the same at home, but that doesn't stop us from trying to recreate the experience. Here are a few dishes that transport us straight to Asia, one smoky bite at a time.

Balinese slow-roasted pork

· SERVES 6–8 ·

This is a very famous dish from Indonesia, which goes by the name *babi guling*, meaning 'roast pork'. Usually a pig around 12 months old is traditionally cooked over hot coals for 3–4 hours. If you get the chance to visit Bali, get along to a *babi guling* restaurant – it's an unforgettable local dining experience. This recipe calls for kencur, which is a ginger-like tuber with a very strong, medicinal flavour. It's easiest to buy it ground from Asian supermarkets. Serve this with plain boiled rice and a nice cold beer!

1.5 kg (3 lb 5 oz) piece boneless pork belly

1½ tablespoons salt

1 teaspoon ground turmeric

1 tablespoon vegetable oil

SPICE PASTE

1½ teaspoons trasi (Indonesian shrimp paste)

3 lemongrass stems, white part only, chopped

5 kaffir lime leaves, central vein removed, finely chopped

3 candlenuts, coarsely chopped

5 brown shallots, coarsely chopped

4 garlic cloves, chopped

6 red bird's eye chillies

1 tablespoon chopped fresh turmeric or
  1 teaspoon ground turmeric

3 cm (1¼ in) piece fresh ginger, chopped

3 teaspoons ground coriander

3 teaspoons ground kencur

1½ tablespoons vegetable oil

TO SERVE

kecap manis

Tomato sambal (see page 19)

peanut crackers (optional)

lime wedges

Using a sharp knife, score the underside of the pork belly all over in a criss-cross pattern, cutting about 1 cm (½ in) into the meat.

For the spice paste, wrap the trasi in foil. Heat a small, heavy-based frying pan over medium heat, add the wrapped trasi then dry-fry for 2 minutes on each side, or until fragrant. Cool and unwrap. Combine with the remaining paste ingredients in a food processor and process until a fairly smooth paste forms. Alternatively, use a mortar and pestle.

Rub the paste all over the scored pork flesh then place in a non-reactive dish, skin side up.

Combine the salt, ground turmeric and oil. Using your fingers, rub this all over the skin of the pork. Refrigerate the meat for 8 hours or overnight for the flavours to develop and the skin to dry out.

Remove the pork from the refrigerator and bring to room temperature. Preheat the oven to 180°C (350°F).

Roast the belly, skin side up, for 25 minutes. Remove the pork from the oven and prick the skin all over with a thin metal skewer, then roast for another 25 minutes.

Heat the oven grill to high and put the pork, skin side up, on an oven tray lined with foil. Cook under the grill, about 8–10 cm (3¼ in–4 in) from the heat, for 10–12 minutes or until the skin is evenly crackled – you may need to rotate the pork to get an even crackling. If you don't have a grill, you can cook the crackling in a 230°C/450°F oven for 15–20 minutes or until crisp.

Stand the pork at room temperature for 10–15 minutes to rest the meat, then slice into 1 cm (½ in) thick pieces. Serve immediately with some kecap manis and tomato sambal for dipping, peanut crackers, if using, and lime wedges for squeezing over.

See image on pages 214–215.

Bun cha

· **SERVES 6** ·

This is a classic dish eaten throughout northern Vietnam – *bun*, meaning 'rice noodles', and *cha*, being 'pork'. On our travels we've witnessed locals regularly packing into their favourite corner cafes, tucking into *bun cha* – and inevitably we joined them.

600 g (1 lb 5 oz) boneless pork shoulder, trimmed, frozen for 90 minutes

600 g (1 lb 5 oz) minced (ground) pork

MARINADE

2½ tablespoons caster (superfine) sugar

2 lemongrass stems, white part only, finely chopped

4 large brown shallots, finely chopped

4 garlic cloves, chopped

1½ teaspoons ground white pepper

2 tablespoons fish sauce

2 teaspoons light soy sauce

60 ml (2 fl oz/¼ cup) vegetable oil

DRESSING

60 ml (2 fl oz/¼ cup) fish sauce

60 ml (2 fl oz/¼ cup) white rice vinegar

2 teaspoons caster (superfine) sugar

1 garlic clove, crushed

1 red bird's eye chilli, finely chopped

TO SERVE

500 g (1 lb 2 oz) thin fresh rice noodles

1 oak leaf or butter lettuce, leaves separated and large ones torn

Pickled carrot (see page 26)

large handful each of Vietnamese mint leaves, mint leaves, coriander (cilantro) leaves and perilla leaves

crushed roasted unsalted peanuts

Spring onion oil (see page 20)

For the marinade, combine the sugar with 2½ tablespoons water in a small saucepan over medium heat and cook, swirling the pan, to dissolve the sugar, about 3–4 minutes. Bring to the boil and cook for 5–6 minutes or until the mixture becomes a deep caramel colour. Remove from the heat and add 2 tablespoons cold water, taking care as the mixture will spit. Cool slightly then add the remaining ingredients and stir to mix well.

Remove the pork from the freezer. Using a large, sharp knife, slice the meat into 3 mm (⅛ in) thick slices. Transfer the meat to a bowl, pour over half the marinade and toss to combine well.

For the dressing, stir all the ingredients together in a bowl with 250 ml (8½ fl oz/1 cup) water, until the sugar has dissolved.

In a separate bowl, combine the remaining marinade with the minced (ground) pork. Using clean hands, work the marinade through the mince. Cover the bowls with plastic wrap and refrigerate for 2 hours, or overnight, for the flavours to develop.

Using your hands, take tablespoonfuls of the mince mixture and form them into flattened discs about 4 cm (1½ in) across.

Heat a barbecue or chargrill pan to medium–high. Cook the patties for about 5 minutes, turning once, or until cooked through. Transfer to a plate and cover with foil to keep warm.

Drain the marinated pork shoulder well. Grill the pork slices for about 4 minutes, turning once, or until lightly charred and cooked through.

Meanwhile, cook the rice noodles according to the packet instructions and drain well. Divide the noodles and lettuce among large bowls. Scatter over some pickled carrot, herbs and peanuts and drizzle over the spring onion oil. Put the patties and pork on top and serve immediately with the dressing on the side.

Coconut grilled chicken

· SERVES 6–8 AS PART OF A SHARED MEAL ·

Cooking this chicken might make a slight mess of your barbecue, but it's completely worth it, especially if you cook it as the Thais do, over coals. This is an easy dish that practically everyone loves. If you feel like cooking a Thai feast, it goes perfectly with a Thai-style salad and rice, plus a curry and a simple stir-fry of leafy vegetables. You can cut each thigh in half before marinating, if you are sharing this among a large number of people. Just reduce the cooking time by 6 minutes.

10 chicken thighs on the bone (about
  2 kg/4 lb 6 oz in total)

6 large dried red chillies, soaked in boiling water
  for 30 minutes, drained

3 lemongrass stems, white part only, chopped

2 teaspoons ground coriander

6 garlic cloves, chopped

2 tablespoons chopped fresh turmeric
  or 2 teaspoons ground turmeric

300 ml (10 fl oz) coconut milk

60 ml (2 fl oz/¼ cup) fish sauce

1 teaspoon ground white pepper

Sweet chilli sauce (see page 15) to serve

lime wedges to serve

Using a large, sharp knife, trim the excess bone of each chicken thigh to give a nice shape. Set aside.

Combine the drained chillies in a food processor with the lemongrass, coriander, garlic and turmeric and process until a smooth paste forms. Alternatively, use a mortar and pestle. Combine with the coconut milk, fish sauce and pepper in a large bowl and add the chicken pieces. Using your hands, turn the chicken to coat well in the mixture. Cover the bowl with plastic wrap and refrigerate for 8 hours or overnight.

Remove the chicken from the refrigerator and bring it to room temperature. Drain the chicken well, reserving the marinade and brushing off any solids.

Heat a barbecue or chargrill pan to medium. Add the chicken and cook, turning occasionally and brushing the chicken with the reserved marinade from time to time, for about 20 minutes or until the chicken is cooked through. Serve with the sweet chilli sauce and lime wedges.

Barbecued five-spice quail

· SERVES 6 AS AN APPETISER OR PART OF A SHARED MEAL ·

The slight gaminess of quail is the perfect counterpoint for a sweet, Vietnamese-style marinade, fragrant with five-spice powder. Serve the quail as an appetiser, or with a selection of other dishes and plenty of steamed rice, as part of a large spread. The quantity of marinade used here could also work for four, butterflied spatchcocks if you prefer, although the cooking time will need to be increased to about 20 minutes.

6 quail (about 1.2 kg/2 lb 10 oz in total)
2 tablespoons vegetable oil, plus extra for cooking
1½ tablespoons soy sauce
3 cm (1¼ in) piece fresh ginger, chopped
2 garlic cloves, chopped
2 tablespoons shaved palm sugar (jaggery)
2 teaspoons five-spice powder
1½ star anise, chopped finely
handful of mint leaves
handful of coriander (cilantro) leaves
handful of perilla leaves, torn
80 g (2¾ oz/½ cup) roasted unsalted peanuts, coarsely chopped

CUCUMBER SALAD
45 g (1½ oz/¼ cup) shaved palm sugar (jaggery)
2 tablespoons lime juice
2 tablespoons rice vinegar
1½ tablespoons fish sauce
4 Lebanese (short) cucumbers, peeled and diced
3 large red Asian shallots, thinly sliced
1 red bird's eye chilli, finely chopped

Using a sharp knife or kitchen scissors, cut through the quail on either side of the backbone, discarding the backbones. Put the quail, skin side up, on a work surface and gently flatten them using the heel of your hand to break the breast bone.

Combine the oil, soy sauce, ginger, garlic cloves, palm sugar and spices in a food processor and process until a paste forms. Alternatively, use a mortar and pestle.

Combine the paste with the quail in a large bowl, turning the quail to coat well. Cover the bowl with plastic wrap and refrigerate for 4 hours or overnight. Drain the quail, reserving the marinade. Season with freshly ground black pepper to taste.

To make the cucumber salad, combine the sugar, lime juice, rice vinegar and fish sauce in a bowl and whisk until the sugar has dissolved. Stir in the cucumber, shallots and chilli, toss to coat well, cover, then stand for 20 minutes.

Heat a barbecue or chargrill pan to medium–high. Cook the quail, in batches if necessary, skin side down, turning once and brushing occasionally with the reserved marinade, for 10 minutes, or until just cooked through – the quail should still be pink in the middle. Transfer the quail to a warmed plate and rest for 5 minutes. Gently scatter over the herbs and the peanuts.

Serve the quail with the cucumber salad on the side.

Honey and pepper lamb

· SERVES 4–6 ·

We're Kiwis so we love lamb. It's in our DNA! Although lamb is one of the less popular meats consumed in Vietnam, it still lends itself to the beautiful flavourings of garlic, lemongrass, fish sauce, sesame and honey, which add an intriguing sweetness to the meat. We like serving this in thin slices as a Vietnamese sandwich, or *banh mi*, filling, but you could also simply have it with rice and salad.

1.2 kg (2 lb 10 oz) boneless lamb leg steaks
   cut into 2.5 cm (1 in) thick slices
1 tablespoon vegetable oil

LAMB MARINADE
6 red Asian shallots, chopped
6 garlic cloves, chopped
2 lemongrass stems, white part only, thinly sliced
50 g (1¾ oz/⅓ cup) sesame seeds
80 g (2¾ oz/⅓ cup) caster (superfine) sugar
2 teaspoons salt
3 teaspoons freshly ground black pepper
2½ tablespoons honey
80 ml (2½ fl oz/⅓ cup) fish sauce
1 tablespoon sesame oil

TO SERVE
large handful of mint leaves
1 iceberg lettuce, thinly sliced
1 telegraph (long) cucumber, peeled
   and thinly sliced
Fried shallots (see page 26)
Pickled carrot (see page 26)
roasted unsalted peanuts
Nuoc cham (see page 16)
Vietnamese baguettes, split open lengthways
mayonnaise for spreading

For the lamb marinade, combine the shallots, garlic and lemongrass in a food processor and process until a coarse paste forms. Alternatively, use a mortar and pestle. Transfer to a large bowl and stir in the remaining ingredients until well combined. Add the lamb steaks and rub the paste evenly over. Cover the bowl tightly with plastic wrap and refrigerate for 3 hours or overnight.

Remove the lamb from the refrigerator and drain well, discarding the marinade, and bring to room temperature.

Preheat a barbecue hotplate or a chargrill pan to medium–high. Brush the lamb with the oil and cook each side for 5–6 minutes, or until cooked through but still a little pink in the middle. Rest for 5 minutes then slice thinly. Serve with all the accompaniments stuffed into split baguettes, spread generously with mayonnaise.

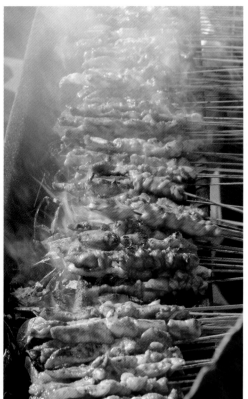

Salt-grilled fish

· **SERVES 4** ·

We've enjoyed this wonderful cooking technique in Laos and Thailand. The salt crust protects the delicate fish from the heat of the barbecue and keeps the juices in. Traditionally an oily fish like mackerel is used, but here we've opted for barramundi. The key to getting the cooking right is to have an even, moderate heat source – not too fierce. Make sure the coals on the barbecue are spread out evenly before you start grilling, or if you are using a chargrill pan, that it conducts heat evenly.

4 lemongrass stems, bruised

4 pandan leaves, trimmed and bruised

4 spring onions (scallions), trimmed and coarsely chopped

12 kaffir lime leaves, bruised

4 x 400 g (14 oz) whole barramundi, snapper or bream, cleaned

60 g (2 oz/½ cup) cornflour (cornstarch)

100 g (3½ oz/¾ cup) coarse sea salt

SAUCE

60 ml (2 fl oz/¼ cup) lime juice

60 ml (2 fl oz/¼ cup) fish sauce

2 tablespoons shaved palm sugar (jaggery)

3 red bird's eye chillies, finely sliced

3 garlic cloves, crushed

TO SERVE

butter lettuce leaves, washed

cherry tomatoes

Thai basil leaves

Vietnamese mint leaves

coriander (cilantro) leaves

200 g (7 oz) thin fresh rice noodles, cooked according to the packet instructions

---

Divide the lemongrass, pandan leaves, spring onion and lime leaves among the fish cavities, then close each cavity using toothpicks or skewers to secure.

Mix the cornflour with 100 ml (3½ fl oz) water to form a thick paste, then brush the mixture lightly over the fish. Coat the outside of each fish with salt, pressing it firmly so it adheres well – each fish should be lightly coated. Stand the fish at room temperature for 30 minutes or until the salt crust feels dry to the touch.

Heat a barbecue or chargrill pan to medium. Add the fish, in batches if necessary, and cook for 15–20 minutes, turning once, or until the flesh is cooked through.

For the sauce, combine all the ingredients in a bowl with 80 ml (2½ fl oz/⅓ cup) water and stir until the sugar has dissolved.

Serve the fish with the lettuce leaves for wrapping, and with the tomatoes, herbs, noodles and sauce in separate bowls.

Roast duck with fermented tofu

· SERVES 4 ·

Known as *chao do* in Vietnamese, this gorgeous dish is very simple to prepare. You will find red fermented tofu in your local Asian supermarket, usually in a glass jar. It adds a unique flavour and a deep, burnished glaze to the duck as well as seasoning the meat. The mixture here can also be brushed over roasting chicken or pork belly, in the same way. Serve this with simple steamed rice garnished with pickled chillies.

1 x 2.2 kg (5 lb) duck

5 pieces red fermented tofu, plus
   2½ tablespoons of the tofu soaking liquid

2½ tablespoons honey

1½ teaspoons five-spice powder

2 cm (¾ in) piece fresh ginger, very finely chopped

1 tablespoon sesame oil

Using paper towel, pat the duck dry all over.

In a large bowl using a fork, mash the fermented tofu well, then combine with the remaining ingredients and mix until smooth.

Add the duck to the bowl and, using your hands, rub the mixture all over the duck to coat, pushing some of the mixture between the skin and flesh where possible, taking care not to tear the skin. Cover the bowl with plastic wrap and refrigerate for 8 hours or overnight.

Bring the duck to room temperature and preheat the oven to 180°C (350°F).

Place the duck on a wire rack inside a roasting tin, breast side down, reserving any marinade and juices left in the bowl. Season well with salt and freshly ground black pepper. Roast for 45 minutes, brushing the duck occasionally with the reserved marinade. Turn the duck over and cook for a further 45 minutes, brushing it occasionally, or until cooked – the juices should still be a little pink when it is pierced between the thigh and the body. Remove the duck from the oven, cover loosely with foil and rest for 20 minutes.

To serve, use a cleaver or large, heavy knife to cut the duck into pieces, through the bone. Place on a platter and serve.

Thai barbecued pork neck

· SERVES 4–6 ·

We love pork neck (also sometimes confusingly called pork butt – but that's another story) and so do the Thais. It's an unctuous, slightly fatty cut, but fat means flavour and it also keeps the meat moist while cooking, so don't trim too much off. *Jaew* in Thailand, or *jeow* in Laos, are ubiquitous dipping sauces, like the one here, which use dried red chillies instead of fresh. Often, toasted rice is also included. As with all dipping sauces, adjust the quantity of ingredients for balance or to your personal taste preference.

6 garlic cloves, crushed

2 tablespoons fish sauce

2 tablespoons dark soy sauce

45 g (1½ oz/¼ cup) shaved palm sugar (jaggery)

2 tablespoons clear rice wine

1 kg (2 lb 3 oz) piece of pork neck, trimmed
   and cut into 1 cm (½ in) slices

1–2 tablespoons vegetable oil

DIPPING SAUCE

1 tablespoon sticky (glutinous) rice

2 lemongrass stems, white part only, finely chopped

6 red Asian shallots, thinly sliced

60 ml (2 fl oz/¼ cup) fish sauce

2 tablespoons light soy sauce

1 tablespoon finely shaved palm sugar (jaggery)

60 ml (2 fl oz/¼ cup) lime juice

3 teaspoons dried chilli flakes

Combine the garlic, fish sauce, soy sauce, palm sugar and rice wine in a bowl and stir until the sugar has dissolved. Add the pork slices and toss to coat. Cover the bowl with plastic wrap and marinate for 8 hours or overnight in the refrigerator.

For the dipping sauce, heat a small, non-stick frying pan over medium–low heat. Add the sticky rice and cook, shaking the pan often, for 6–7 minutes or until golden. Cool. Transfer to an electric spice grinder and grind to a coarse powder. Alternatively, use a mortar and pestle. Combine with the remaining ingredients in a bowl, stirring until the sugar has dissolved.

Drain the pork well, reserving the marinade.

Preheat a barbecue or chargrill pan to medium–high and add 1 tablespoon of the oil. Add the pork slices, in batches (using the extra oil if necessary), and cook, basting with the reserved marinade and turning once, for 4–5 minutes each side, or until cooked through. Season with freshly ground black pepper, if desired, and transfer to a platter. Cover loosely with foil to keep warm. Serve with the dipping sauce on the side.

Lime leaf grilled chicken

· **SERVES 4–6** ·

Years ago we attended a cooking class given by French chef Didier Corlou, who has made Hanoi his home for decades. He used lemon leaves for this dish, but kaffir lime leaves work deliciously well too. In Vietnam you'd grill these in the long bamboo pincers that are commonly used to hold meat, fish or other foods in place over hot coals – which we swear add another layer of flavour. Skewers are just fine though. Don't worry if you lose a leaf or two in the process – the chicken will still taste sublime.

10 boneless, skinless chicken thighs
(about 1.1 kg/2 lb 7 oz), excess fat removed
30 large double kaffir lime leaves
10 wooden skewers, soaked in water
for 30 minutes
vegetable oil for cooking
Nuoc cham (see page 16) to serve

MARINADE

1 tablespoon very finely chopped fresh turmeric
or 1 teaspoon ground turmeric
1 large pinch of ground turmeric
4 garlic cloves, finely chopped
1 tablespoon caster (superfine) sugar
2½ tablespoons fish sauce
10 kaffir lime leaves, central vein removed,
finely chopped
1 teaspoon ground white pepper

For the marinade, combine all the ingredients in a food processor and process until a coarse paste forms. Alternatively, use a mortar and pestle.

Cut each chicken thigh into 3 even-sized pieces crossways. Combine in a bowl with the paste and use your hands to coat the chicken well. Cover and refrigerate for 2 hours or overnight.

Wrap each piece of chicken in a double lime leaf, threading each piece onto two skewers as you wrap them, taking care to secure both the leaf and the chicken. Thread 3 pieces of chicken onto each double skewer.

Heat a barbecue or chargrill pan to medium. Brush the wrapped chicken pieces all over with oil and cook for 8 minutes, turning occasionally, or until the leaves are charred and the chicken is just cooked through. Serve with the nuoc cham for dipping.

Coconut-glazed beef ribs

· SERVES 4–6 ·

We love this recipe – it's beef, it's ribs, it's tender, it's charred, it's sticky, it's got a touch of heat, and the lime cuts through the richness for balance. What's not to love? The coconut stock imparts a lush, rich element to the ribs, but remember to simmer them until they're nice and tender, and watch the glazing process, as they can easily burn at this stage. Perfect this recipe and you will have constant requests from friends and family to cook it for them, we promise.

2 kg (4 lb 6 oz) beef short ribs, cut into approximately 12 cm (4¾ in) lengths (ask your butcher to do this)
2 lemongrass stems, bruised
2 x 8 cm (3¼ in) pieces fresh galangal, sliced
2 long red chillies, chopped
1 litre (34 fl oz/4 cups) coconut milk
250 ml (8½ fl oz/1 cup) fish sauce
150 g (5½ oz) shaved palm sugar (jaggery)
thinly sliced medium red chilli to serve

COCONUT CREAM GLAZE
2½ tablespoons shaved palm sugar (jaggery)
100 ml (3½ fl oz) fish sauce
1 lemongrass stem, white part only, chopped
6 kaffir lime leaves
6 red Asian shallots, chopped
100 ml (3½ fl oz) coconut cream

Combine the ribs, lemongrass, galangal, chillies, coconut milk, fish sauce, palm sugar and 1 litre (34 fl oz/4 cups) cold water in a large saucepan over medium heat, adding more water to cover the ribs if necessary. Bring to the boil then reduce the heat to low and simmer for 3 hours, regularly skimming the impurities that rise to the surface, or until the meat is tender and starting to fall off the bones. Remove the pan from the heat and cool the ribs in the liquid. Remove the ribs from the liquid, reserving the liquid for soup or another use.

Heat a barbecue or chargrill pan to medium–high.

For the glaze, combine the palm sugar, fish sauce, lemongrass, lime leaves and shallots in a small saucepan over medium heat and bring to a simmer. Cook for 5 minutes or until well combined and slightly syrupy. Strain the mixture, discarding the solids.

Divide the mixture in two, combining one half in a bowl with the coconut cream and reserving the other. Carefully coat the ribs with the reserved half of the glaze, using a brush.

Put the short ribs, meat side down, on the barbecue and cook for 10–15 minutes turning every 5 minutes and basting with the syrup, or until the ribs are well glazed and sticky. Remove and rest for 10 minutes. Either leave the ribs whole or cut them into smaller pieces.

Place the meat on a platter and serve with the coconut cream glaze and the sliced chilli on the side.

Slow-roasted lamb

· **SERVES 6–8** ·

Domestic stoves are not common in traditional Asian kitchens, although that's rapidly changing as the region grows, develops and succumbs to Western influence. We've taken a more contemporary Indonesian approach here, as it does require an oven. Plus, we've nodded to our Antipodean roots – we can't help ourselves, as we love lamb. Lamb shoulder on the bone gives great flavour as it contains a decent amount of fat.

2 x 1.5 kg (3 lb 5 oz) lamb shoulders

8 garlic cloves, crushed

1 tablespoon finely chopped fresh ginger

1 tablespoon chopped fresh turmeric or
   1 teaspoon ground turmeric

1 lemongrass stem, white part only, finely chopped

2 teaspoons freshly ground black pepper

2 tablespoons vegetable oil

GREEN MANGO SAMBAL

2½ teaspoons trasi (Indonesian shrimp paste)

5 red bird's eye chillies

2 tablespoons shaved palm sugar (jaggery)

2 green mangoes, peeled and flesh finely shredded

1 tomato, finely chopped

COCONUT CHILLI SAMBAL

3 red bird's eye chillies, chopped

4 red Asian shallots, chopped

1 garlic clove, chopped

2 kaffir lime leaves, central vein
   removed, shredded

150 g (5½ oz/1½ cups) fresh grated or thawed frozen
   grated coconut (see page 28)

2 teaspoons sugar

Trim any excess fat from the lamb. Using a small, sharp knife, make 2 cm (¾ in) deep incisions all over the meat.

Combine the garlic, ginger, turmeric, lemongrass and pepper in a food processor and process until a fine paste forms. Push the mixture into the incisions in the lamb, rubbing any excess paste over the surface of the meat. Put the lamb in a large bowl, cover with plastic wrap and stand at cool room temperature for 1–2 hours, or refrigerate for 2 hours or overnight. If the lamb has been refrigerated, bring it to room temperature.

Preheat the oven to 160°C (320°F). Rub the lamb all over with oil and season with salt. Place in a roasting tin and cook for 5 hours or until very tender.

Meanwhile for the green mango sambal, wrap the trasi in foil. Heat a small, heavy-based frying pan over medium heat, add the wrapped trasi then dry-fry for 2 minutes on each side, or until fragrant. Cool and unwrap. Combine 2 teaspoons of the trasi in a food processor with the chillies and sugar and process until a coarse paste forms. Alternatively, use a mortar and pestle. Combine with the mango and tomato in a bowl then, using clean hands, massage the paste and tomato into the mango. Season with salt and freshly ground black pepper.

For the coconut chilli sambal, combine the remaining trasi, chillies, shallots, garlic and kaffir lime leaves in a food processor and process until a coarse paste forms. Alternatively, use a mortar and pestle. Combine with the coconut and sugar and mix well. Season to taste with salt and freshly ground black pepper then cover and stand for 20 minutes to allow the flavours to develop. Serve the meat in chunks with the sambals on the side.

Desserts

Light, refreshing and pulling flavour punches
from all kinds of unexpected quarters, Asian
sweets are our preferred type of dessert.
They're fragranced with pandan, spiked with
ginger, made sticky with palm sugar (jaggery)
and loaded with textural interest from mung
beans, grated coconut, sesame seeds and more.
They're not strictly puddings, though, as sweet
treats in Asia are eaten throughout the day
as pick-me-up snacks. Sugar banana cake or
coconut pandan pancakes could just as easily
be served at breakfast so eat them, and the rest
of these dishes, whenever the mood takes you!

Tropical fruit with star anise ice cream

· SERVES 6 ·

This recipe falls into the 'inspired by' category, rather than the truly authentic. No matter, as it's delicious, light and easy to put together. A visit to any Southeast Asian country will quickly show how much ice cream is loved there. In Thailand, vendors sell fantastic home-made coconut ice cream (and sometimes mango), made with coconut milk, which is lighter and more refreshing than dairy-based ice cream. Here we've gone for a dairy ice cream but made with the surprisingly gorgeous flavour of star anise. The colour is amazing, too!

½ rockmelon (cantaloupe/netted melon), peeled, seeded and thinly sliced

3 sugar bananas, cut into 2 cm (¾ in) pieces

½ ripe, medium pineapple, peeled, eyes removed, cored and cut into bite-sized chunks

1 large, ripe mango, peeled, seeded and cut into bite-sized chunks

STAR ANISE ICE CREAM
2 star anise

350 ml (12 fl oz) milk

500 ml (17 fl oz/2 cups) pouring (single/light) cream

6 egg yolks

230 g (8 oz/1 cup firmly packed) dark brown sugar

LIME AND LEMONGRASS SYRUP
180 g (6½ oz/1 cup) shaved light palm sugar (jaggery)

125 ml (4 fl oz/½ cup) lime juice

2½ tablespoons clear rice wine

2 lemongrass stems, white part only, thinly sliced

4 kaffir lime leaves, central vein removed, thinly sliced

For the star anise ice cream, dry-fry the star anise in a small frying pan over medium heat, shaking the pan often, for 5 minutes or until fragrant. Transfer to an electric spice grinder and grind to a fine powder.

Combine the milk and cream in a saucepan over medium heat, bring almost to a simmer then remove from the heat. Stir in the ground star anise. Using hand-held electric beaters, whisk the egg yolks and sugar until thick and pale, pour the milk mixture over and stir to combine well.

Return the mixture to a clean pan and stir constantly over medium–low heat until the mixture thickens enough to just coat the back of a wooden spoon – do not let the mixture get too hot or it will curdle. Remove from the heat, cool to room temperature and refrigerate until chilled. Transfer to an ice cream machine and churn according to the manufacturer's instructions. (The ice cream will keep, covered in the freezer, for up to 5 days.)

For the lime and lemongrass syrup, combine all the ingredients with 125 ml (4 fl oz/½ cup) water in a saucepan over medium heat. Bring to the boil, reduce the heat to low and simmer, stirring, for 5 minutes or until the sugar has dissolved. Remove from the heat and cool to room temperature. Strain, if desired, discarding the solids.

Divide the fruit among serving bowls, spoon the syrup over and serve with the ice cream.

See image on pages 240–241.

Sweet beans with coconut sticky rice

· **SERVES 6** ·

Sweetened vegetable and rice combinations for dessert might seem strange, but beans, corn, taro and sweet potato are widely used in Asian sweets. This Vietnamese-inspired dessert – a sweetened variation of the hefty street fare dish called *xoi*, which Hanoians eat for breakfast – combines a pleasing blend of textures and flavours. You can assemble the dessert for your guests, or serve the rice in small bowls and allow diners to add the sweet beans, coconut, sesame seeds and coconut milk to taste.

110 g (4 oz/½ cup) adzuki beans, soaked overnight in water to cover, drained

145 g (5 oz/⅔ cup) caster (superfine) sugar

350 g (12½ oz/1¾ cups) sticky (glutinous) rice, soaked overnight in water to cover, drained well

600 ml (20½ fl oz) coconut milk

½ teaspoon salt

TO SERVE

fresh grated or thawed frozen grated coconut (see page 28)

40 g (1½ oz/¼ cup) toasted sesame seeds

Put the adzuki beans in a small saucepan over medium–high heat with 500 ml (17 fl oz/2 cups) water or enough to cover the beans. Bring to the boil then reduce the heat to medium–low and simmer, skimming any impurities that rise to the surface, for about 25 minutes or until the beans are soft. Add half the sugar, bring back to a simmer and cook the mixture over medium heat for 20 minutes or until the liquid is reduced and syrupy. Remove from the heat and cool.

Meanwhile, spread the rice evenly over a steamer lined with a clean, damp tea (dish) towel and steam, covered, over boiling water for 20 minutes or until just cooked. Transfer the rice to a bowl.

Combine 190 ml (6½ fl oz/¾ cup) of the coconut milk with the remaining sugar and the salt in a small saucepan over medium heat and cook until the sugar has dissolved. Transfer to the bowl with the rice. Stir gently to combine then cool to room temperature.

Divide the rice mixture among serving bowls, top with the bean mixture, coconut and sesame seeds, serving the remaining coconut milk separately.

Sugar banana cake

· **SERVES 8** ·

The ubiquitous cavendish banana is positively bland compared to the taste of lady fingers and the other small varieties of banana, which are prevalent throughout Southeast Asia. With their dense texture and intense tang, lady fingers hit all kinds of satisfying notes that our common garden bananas just don't. Sugar bananas also work well here, with their sweet flavour and the way they hold their shape during cooking. This light cake benefits from chilling, so it can be easily and neatly sliced.

250 ml (8½ fl oz/1 cup) coconut milk

60 ml (2 fl oz/¼ cup) sweetened condensed milk

150 g (5½ oz) caster (superfine) sugar

1 regular baguette, crusts removed and cut into 5 mm (¼ in) slices or 3-day-old Vietnamese baguette rolls (about 300 g/10½ oz bread in total)

650 g (1 lb 7 oz) sugar bananas (about 5) peeled and cut lengthways into 5 mm (¼ in) slices

20 g (¾ oz) unsalted butter, plus extra for greasing

coconut cream to serve

Combine the coconut milk, condensed milk and all but 2 tablespoons of the sugar in a small saucepan over medium–low heat. Stir until the sugar has dissolved, then remove from the heat and cool slightly.

Preheat the oven to 180°C (350°F) and lightly grease the base and side of a 19 cm (7½ in) springform cake tin.

Briefly dip a third of the baguette slices in the milk mixture and use them to line the base of the tin. Cover the bread slices evenly with a third of the banana slices then continue layering until the bread and banana are all used, finishing with a layer of banana. Dot the surface of the cake with butter, sprinkle with the remaining sugar then bake for 1 hour or until golden and firm. Cool the cake in the tin then refrigerate for 4 hours or overnight.

Serve wedges of the cake with the coconut cream on the side for pouring over.

Mung bean dumplings

· SERVES 6 ·

Rice and sticky (glutinous) rice flour are used extensively in Asian desserts, and here they are both employed in a dough that, when cooked, is light and delightfully chewy. The pleasant heat of fresh ginger infuses the sweet broth – use more or less as the mood takes you. Cook these just before you plan to eat them as, while they will hold for an hour or so, they don't take well to sitting around for too long once cooked. Use light-coloured palm sugar for the syrup, as you want a more neutural flavour than the dark variety would add.

100 g (3½ oz/½ cup) dried split mung beans, soaked overnight in water to cover, drained
125 ml (4 fl oz/½ cup) coconut milk
2 teaspoons caster (superfine) sugar
2 teaspoons peanut oil
265 g (9½ oz/1½ cups) sticky (glutinous) rice flour

265 g (9½ oz/1½ cups) rice flour
300 ml (10 fl oz) hot water
325 g (11½ oz) palm sugar (jaggery), chopped
5 cm (2 in) piece fresh ginger, cut into fine matchsticks
40 g (1½ oz/¼ cup) toasted sesame seeds
coconut cream, to serve

Combine the drained mung beans, coconut milk and 125 ml (4 fl oz/½ cup) water in a small saucepan over medium–low heat and bring to a simmer. Cook, covered, over low heat for 20 minutes or until the water is absorbed and the beans are very tender. Add the caster sugar and oil and stir to break up the beans and form a coarse paste. Cool the mixture to room temperature then refrigerate for 2 hours or until firm.

Combine the rice flours in a bowl then, stirring continuously with a fork, add all but around 1½ tablespoons of the hot water to the flours, adding only as much of the remaining water as you need. Continue stirring until the mixture is firm and comes away from the side of the bowl. Cover the dough with a damp cloth and rest for 20 minutes.

While the dough rests, take ½ tablespoonfuls of the mung bean mixture and use your hands to form it into 18 balls.

Combine the palm sugar, ginger and 625 ml (21 fl oz/2½ cups) water in a saucepan and bring to the boil over medium heat, stirring until the sugar has dissolved. Reduce the heat to low and cover to keep the mixture hot.

Divide the dough into 18 even-sized pieces and roll each into a ball. Using oiled hands, form each ball into a disc about 9 cm (3½ in) across. With a dough disc in one hand, place a ball of mung bean filling in the centre. Then, using your other hand, draw the edges of the dough disc up over the filling to enclose it, pressing the edges to seal and patching any holes in the dough as you go. Repeat the process with the remaining dough and mung bean balls.

Bring a large saucepan of water to the boil over medium–high heat. Cook the dumplings in the boiling water, in batches, for 8–10 minutes, then transfer to the ginger syrup in the saucepan.

Divide the dumplings among serving bowls. Spoon over the ginger syrup, sprinkle with the sesame seeds and serve immediately with a splash of coconut cream.

Pandan and rose sago jellies

· MAKES ABOUT 28 ·

Sago is a starchy substance processed from the pith of a species of palm and it's commonly used in Southeast Asian desserts. It's either processed into a powder or into small white balls, as used here. It really doesn't have much (if any) taste of its own, but it readily takes on other flavours – and colours too. These jellies are best eaten the day they are made, as they don't take well to refrigeration, turning rubbery and a little hard.

300 g (10½ oz) sago (tapioca) pearls
1½ tablespoons cornflour (cornstarch)
145 g (5 oz/⅔ cup) caster (superfine) sugar
80 ml (2½ fl oz/⅓ cup) pandan juice (see page 29)

1½ tablespoons rose syrup
fresh grated or thawed frozen grated coconut
  (see page 28) for coating

Soak the sago in a bowl of water to cover for 1 hour. Drain well then divide it in half.

Bring a large saucepan of water, fitted with a steamer, to the boil. Put one half of the sago in a bowl large enough to fit inside the steamer then add 3½ teaspoons of the cornflour, half the sugar and the pandan juice. Stir to mix well then put the bowl in the steamer. Cover tightly and steam for 35–40 minutes or until the mixture is very thick and translucent.

In another bowl, combine the remaining sago, remaining cornflour, remaining sugar and rose syrup and stir to mix well. Steam for 35–40 minutes or until cooked.

Cool each bowl of sago slightly then turn out onto a board. Using a sharp, wet knife, cut each into 14 even-sized pieces. Roll each piece in the coconut to coat well and serve.

Pumpkin rice balls

· **SERVES 4** ·

Asian desserts are light, generally not too sweet and downright intriguing in their use of vegetables, pulses, herbs and other components foreign to Western sweet cookery. However, pumpkin, as used in this dish, is probably not that unusual a dessert ingredient, as it's also used in a few European, Latin and American sweets. Use a pumpkin variety that's got plenty of good flavour and is not too wet in texture. We generally favour jap pumpkins in most of our cooking.

250 g (9 oz) jap pumpkin (kabocha), peeled and seeded
235 g (8½ oz/1⅓ cups) rice flour
3 pandan leaves
115 g (4 oz/½ cup) caster (superfine) sugar

500 ml (17 fl oz/2 cups) coconut milk
large pinch of salt

Cut the pumpkin into 2 cm (¾ in) pieces then steam for 8–9 minutes or until tender. Transfer to a food processor and process until very smooth. Cool slightly.

Measure 185 g (6½ oz/¾ cup) pumpkin and combine in a large bowl with the rice flour then stir until a firm dough forms. Knead lightly, then cover with plastic wrap until ready to use.

Meanwhile, bruise the pandan leaves and tear into 6 cm (2½ in) pieces. Put them in a saucepan over medium heat with the sugar and 125 ml (4 fl oz/½ cup) water. Cover, bring to a simmer and cook, stirring occasionally to dissolve the sugar, for 5–6 minutes. Remove from the heat and stand for 30 minutes to infuse. Strain the mixture and discard the solids.

Over low heat, stir the coconut milk and salt into the pandan liquid, but do not let it simmer. Cover and keep warm.

Bring a large saucepan of water to the boil. Form teaspoonfuls of the pumpkin mixture into balls then add to the boiling water, in batches, and cook for 3–4 minutes or until they rise to the surface. Transfer to serving bowls using a slotted spoon, draining well. Pour some of the warm coconut milk mixture over the balls in each bowl and serve immediately.

Rice and palm sugar cake

· MAKES 12 PIECES ·

The Thais make amazing desserts. Locally known as *khanom*, they form a much-loved part of their diet. For this recipe, feel free to use clear pandan essence (not the lurid green stuff) instead of the pandan leaves, if it's easier and more accessible. Around 1 teaspoon should do it, but add it a little at a time until you reach your desired taste. Southeast Asian and Indian shops sell the essence, or frozen pandan leaves are also fine to use.

400 g (14 oz/2 cups) sticky (glutinous) rice, soaked overnight in water to cover, drained well
250 ml (8½ oz/1 cup) coconut milk

225 g (8 oz/1¼ cups) shaved palm sugar (jaggery)
3 pandan leaves, bruised, tied together in a knot

Bring a saucepan of water, fitted with a steamer, to the boil over high heat. Line the steamer with a clean tea (dish) towel. Put the rice in the tea towel, folding it over to enclose the rice. Cover the pan tightly and cook for 20–25 minutes or until the rice is tender. Unwrap the rice and transfer it to a bowl.

Meanwhile, combine the coconut milk, palm sugar and pandan leaves in a large saucepan and bring to a simmer over medium–low heat. Cover and cook, stirring occasionally, for 10 minutes or until the sugar has dissolved and the mixture is well infused. Discard the pandan leaves, add the rice and cook, stirring gently every now and then to break up the rice, for 12–15 minutes or until the rice has absorbed the liquid. Cool slightly.

Lightly oil the base and side of a 19 cm (7½ in) cake tin and line with baking paper.

When cool enough to handle, transfer the rice to the tin, using wet hands to press it evenly into the tin. Cover the tin with plastic wrap, then stand at room temperature for 1 hour or until completely cooled.

Turn the rice out onto a chopping board and, using a wet knife as the rice is very sticky, cut it into 4 x 4 cm (1¾ x 1¾ in) pieces and serve.

Soy milk jellies with coffee syrup

· SERVES 6 ·

Unusually for an Asian nation, the Vietnamese have a fondness for coffee – a taste they acquired from their French colonisers. (Interestingly, Vietnam supplies the world coffee trade with much of its robusta beans, most of which end up as instant coffee.) The Vietnamese enjoy their coffee strong and sweet, commonly serving it with lashings of condensed milk. Inspired by those flavours, this simple dessert is a wonderful combination of soothing, barely set milky jelly with the jolt of a strong, coffee-based syrup. The left-over syrup keeps well and tastes delicious spooned over ice cream.

2½ teaspoons powdered gelatine
160 ml (5½ fl oz) sweetened condensed milk
330 ml (11 fl oz) soy milk

270 g (9½ oz/1½ cups) chopped palm sugar (jaggery)
25 g (1 oz/⅓ cup) coarsely ground coffee beans

Sprinkle the gelatine over 2 tablespoons cold water in a cup or small bowl and stand for 5 minutes or until softened.

Meanwhile, combine the condensed and soy milks in a small saucepan and gently heat over medium–low heat – do not simmer. Stir in the gelatine mixture and cook, stirring, for 2 minutes or until the gelatine has dissolved. Cool to room temperature. Divide among six 175 ml (6 fl oz) glasses or serving bowls and refrigerate for 6 hours or overnight – the jellies will just be lightly set.

Combine the palm sugar and 400 ml (13½ fl oz) water in a small saucepan and slowly bring to the boil over medium heat, stirring until the sugar has dissolved. Reduce the heat to low and simmer

for 5 minutes or until slightly thickened. Add the coffee and cook for another 2 minutes for the flavours to infuse. Remove from the heat and cool to room temperature.

Strain the syrup through a fine-mesh sieve, discarding the solids, then refrigerate until cold.

Pour some of the syrup over the jellies and serve with the remaining syrup on the side.

Coconut pandan pancakes

· MAKES 6 ·

These delicious pancakes are a traditional sweet from Bali, most commonly eaten for breakfast, but they also make a fantastic dessert. Make the pancakes and filling in advance, then assemble them just before you plan to serve and scoff them. If you can't get fresh pandan leaves for the pancakes, substitute 1 teaspoon pandan paste, which you can easily purchase from Asian or Indian food stores. Be warned though, it will make the pancakes very green!

5 pandan leaves, chopped
100 ml (3½ fl oz) coconut milk
1 egg
150 g (5½ oz/1 cup) plain (all-purpose) flour
large pinch of salt
vegetable oil for cooking

FILLING

90 g (3 oz/½ cup) shaved palm sugar (jaggery)
150 g (5½ oz/1½ cups) fresh grated or frozen thawed grated coconut (see page 28)

For the filling, combine the palm sugar and 80 ml (2½ fl oz/⅓ cup) water in a small saucepan over medium heat. Bring to a simmer and cook, stirring occasionally, for 4 minutes or until the sugar has dissolved. Transfer to a bowl and cool to room temperature. Add the coconut and stir to combine well.

Meanwhile, combine the pandan leaves and 200 ml (7 fl oz) water in a food processor and process until the leaves are very finely chopped and the liquid is green. Transfer to a sieve placed over a bowl and strain the mixture well, pushing down on the pandan with your hands to extract as much liquid as possible. Discard the solids.

Combine the pandan liquid, coconut milk, egg, flour and salt in a food processor and process until a smooth, thin batter forms, adding a little water if the mixture is too thick (it should lightly coat the back of a spoon).

Heat a 16 cm (6¼ in) non-stick frying pan or crêpe pan over medium–high heat and brush lightly with oil. Add about 2½ tablespoons of the batter to the pan, or enough to thinly coat the base, working quickly and swirling the pan to coat it evenly. Cook for 2 minutes or until the pancake looks dry on top, then turn over and cook for another 1–2 minutes or until cooked through. Transfer to a plate. Repeat with the remaining mixture, brushing the pan with a little extra oil if necessary, and adding a little more water to the batter if it thickens on standing.

Divide the coconut filling among the pancakes, placing it in a neat line, about 9 cm (3½ in) long, in the middle of each. Fold the sides of each pancake over the filling, then neatly roll up to form a log. Serve with any left-over filling on the side.

Mung bean custard

· SERVES 8–10 ·

There's a school of thought suggesting desserts like this were introduced into the Siamese court during the seventeenth century by a Portuguese woman called Maria Guyomar de Pinha. It's a longer story than we have room for here, but suffice to say, this custard-style dessert, with its unmistakably Thai touches, is totally delicious. It's our kind of treat.

150 g (5½ oz/¾ cup) dried split mung beans, soaked in cold water overnight
vegetable oil for greasing
230 g (8 oz/1 cup) caster (superfine) sugar
6 large eggs, lightly beaten

2 tablespoons cornflour (cornstarch)
250 ml (8½ fl oz/1 cup) coconut milk
½ teaspoon salt
Fried shallots (page 26) to serve

Combine the dried mung beans with enough water to cover in a saucepan over medium heat and bring to the boil. Cover and cook, adding a little more water as necessary to keep the beans covered, for 40 minutes or until the beans are very tender. Drain well and cool slightly.

Preheat the oven to 180°C (350°C) and lightly grease a 15 x 15 x 5 cm (6 x 6 x 2 in) baking dish with vegetable oil.

Transfer the beans to a food processor and process until smooth. Add the remaining ingredients, except the fried shallots, and process until very smooth and well combined. Pour into the prepared dish, smoothing the top. Bake for 1 hour or until firm and deep golden. Remove from the oven.

Cool the custard to room temperature then cut it into 6 x 3 cm (2½ x 1¼ in) pieces. Sprinkle each piece with the fried shallots and serve. This will keep refrigerated for 2–3 days, covered with plastic wrap.

Coconut custard with black sticky rice

· SERVES 6 ·

Asian desserts are as much about texture and flavour, as they are about boosting energy levels, which flag in unrelenting tropical heat. Here, smooth custard meets the toothsome, sweet grains of black sticky rice and slices of mango – one of the sexiest fruits around. As avowed durian lovers, we'd also entertain the idea of using that fruit instead, but realise we're probably in the minority – among our non-Asian friends at least! – due to its unusual fragrance.

180 g (6½ oz/1 cup) light palm sugar (jaggery), chopped
375 ml (12½ fl oz/1½ cups) coconut milk
4 eggs, well beaten
½ teaspoon salt

BLACK STICKY RICE
300 g (10½ oz/1½ cups) black sticky (glutinous) rice
4 pandan leaves, bruised and tied in a knot
60 g (2 oz/⅓ cup) shaved palm sugar (jaggery)
125 ml (4 fl oz/½ cup) coconut milk

TO SERVE
2 large ripe mangoes, peeled, stoned and sliced
toasted sesame seeds

For the black sticky rice, put the rice in a large bowl and add enough water to cover. Soak for 8 hours or overnight. Drain well.

Put the rice in a bowl, add enough water to barely cover the rice then add the pandan leaves. Put the bowl in a steamer, cover and cook for 45 minutes or until the rice is tender. Remove from the heat. Drain well and discard the pandan leaves. Add the palm sugar and a large pinch of salt and transfer to a clean bowl. Stir until the sugar has dissolved. Add the coconut milk, stir to combine well and leave to cool to room temperature.

Combine the light palm sugar with 80 ml (2½ fl oz/⅓ cup) water in a small saucepan. Bring to a simmer over medium heat then cover and cook, stirring occasionally, for 5 minutes or until the sugar has dissolved. Cool slightly.

Bring a large steamer to the boil.

In a bowl, whisk together the sugar mixture, coconut milk, eggs and salt. Pour into a 1.25 litre (42 fl oz/5 cup) capacity heatproof bowl and cover the bowl with a saucepan lid or similar. Put the bowl in the steamer and cook over medium heat for 40 minutes or until the custard is set but still a little wobbly in the centre – take care not to overcook or the custard will develop holes. Cool to room temperature.

Serve the custard in scoops with the black sticky rice and mango slices and the sesame seeds scattered over.

Glossary

annatto oil is a red-orange cooking oil with a slight sweet, peppery flavour. Available from Asian supermarkets, it is largely used in some Vietnamese dishes to impart colour.

betel leaves are glossy, heart-shaped, edible leaves from a plant that belongs to the same botanical family as pepper. They have many uses, but are popularly used raw as a wrapper for the Thai snack dish, *miang*.

bitter melon, or bitter gourd, lives up to its name, as it is very bitter in flavour. It is related to the cucumber and is appreciated for its culinary uses and its medicinal properties.

cakwe, also known as *youtiao*, or Chinese doughnuts, are long, cylindrical strips of dough, which are deep-fried and served alongside dishes like rice porridges. You can buy these in packets from Chinese supermarkets or fresh from a Chinese congee restaurant.

candlenuts are hard nuts from a flowering tree, which have a high oil content. They are used, ground, to thicken (mainly) Malaysian and Indonesian curries. They are toxic raw, so should always be cooked.

cha om (acacia leaf) are the young leaves of a variety of climbing wattle that's found throughout Southeast Asia. The leaves have a strong smell, which settles down once cooked – the flavour is also distinctive. The leaves are used in omelettes, soups, salads, curries and stir-fries and can sometimes be found fresh in Thai supermarkets. They are also sold in frozen blocks.

Chinese barbecued duck, or roast duck, is air-dried duck, usually seasoned with five-spice powder and sugar, then roasted – although there are many variations. These tend to be the glistening ducks you see hanging in Chinese restaurant windows.

Chinese barbecued pork, or *char siu*, is a famous sweet and sticky roasted pork dish, glazed with a combination of honey, five-spice powder, soy sauce, hoisin sauce and sometimes red food colouring.

Chinese cabbage (wombok) is an oval-shaped cabbage with a mild and slightly sweet flavour. It can be used in salads, steamed or stir-fried.

Chinese celery is finer and more delicate-tasting than common celery. The hollow stalks, as well as the leaves, are usually used to flavour stir-fries, noodle dishes and soups. Buy it from Chinese or Asian greengrocers.

Chinese mushrooms refers to various types of fresh and dried Asian mushrooms, such as shiitake, enoki and oyster mushrooms and dried black fungus (wood ears). Dried shiitake mushrooms are a staple of many Southeast Asian cuisines and are commonly found in Chinese supermarkets. They must be soaked to rehydrate them before using. Where they are specified in a recipe, there really aren't any suitable alternatives to their unique, umami flavour.

Chinese sausages, or *lap cheong*, are cured, dried, pork-based sausages, which contain a fair amount of fat. They are used throughout Southeast Asia, especially in areas with a historic Chinese influence. You will find them in Chinese or Asian supermarkets in the dry-goods section in vacuum packs.

choy sum is a green leafy vegetable similar to bok choy, used in braises, soups, stir-fries and steamed dishes.

claypot is a cooking vessel as well as a technique, usually involving a pot made of unglazed clay. These pots keep moisture and flavour in a dish, and can be used on the stovetop or in an oven. They require soaking in water before being used for the first time.

coconut milk and cream are made by blending the flesh of a coconut with water, then straining it hard through a cloth, or similar, to remove as much liquid as possible. When allowed to stand, coconut cream will rise to the top – the liquid underneath is coconut milk. Coconut water is the clear, light-flavoured liquid that comes from a young coconut. While it is possible to make your own coconut milk and cream, it is more convenient to buy it – always be sure to buy a quality brand. Coconut water can be purchased frozen from Asian supermarkets, or you can use the fresh water from green coconuts (available from Asian greengrocers and health food stores).

curry leaves are the small, green and very aromatic leaves of the curry tree, which add flavour and colour to Indian-influenced dishes. As such, they are widely used in Malaysian cookery. Buy them fresh or frozen from a greengrocer or an Indian supermarket.

dried shrimp are sun-dried and rather hard prawns (shrimp). They come available in different sizes and have a concentrated flavour – not many are needed to flavour a dish. They keep well, refrigerated or frozen. Generally they are used finely ground or are first soaked to soften them, then either used whole or chopped. They're used in many dishes, including sambals, soups, salads, sauces, stir-fries, braises and in steamed and fried snacks.

fermented black beans, also known as salted or dried black beans, are a strongly flavoured and common Chinese ingredient. The beans are fermented with salt, so generally need to be rinsed or even soaked before using to reduce saltiness.

fermented soy bean sauce is a reddish-brown sauce made from soy beans. The sauce is salty and can be spicy with the addition of chilli. It is typically used as a side dish or in braises, soups and stir-fries.

fish balls are firm and slightly rubbery balls made from a fine fish paste. They are used as an ingredient in soups, certain curries, noodle dishes, hot pots and on skewers. Conveniently, they can be purchased, already cooked, from the refrigerator section of Asian and Chinese supermarkets. They just need reheating.

galangal is a hard rhizome, which belongs to the same family as ginger, and is used both in cooking and for medicinal purposes throughout Southeast Asia. It has a distinctive flavour, which can't really be substituted. You will find it fresh in Chinese or Asian greengrocers and some supermarkets.

jicama is a large, tuberous root vegetable with brown skin and white crunchy flesh, which can be eaten raw as well as cooked. Also called yam bean, it is particularly delicious in salads and as part of a plate of raw vegetables to accompany dips and other snacks.

kaffir lime leaves come from the kaffir lime tree, found throughout Southeast Asia. The leaves are highly aromatic and are distinctive as they have double leaf lobes. In this book, '1 kaffir lime leaf' refers to 1 double leaf. They are used in various dishes, including curries, salads, steamed dishes and soups, and are also used as a fragrant garnish, finely shredded.

kecap manis is a sweet, thick soy sauce flavoured with palm sugar (jaggery). Originating in Indonesia, it is used primarily as a condiment, but also finds its way into myriad recipes as a sweetening agent. There is also a Thai sweet soy sauce, which is similar.

mam nem is a Vietnamese fermented shrimp sauce, usually made from small prawns (shrimp). These are sun-dried then ground, salt and sugar are added and then the prawns are left to ferment to produce a pungent, pinkish-grey, thick paste. Buy it in bottles from Asian supermarkets.

mustard greens, or mustard plant, is a large, leafy green from the brassica family. It resembles a type of kale, but has a distinct mustard flavour. It can be eaten raw or added to cooked dishes, equally popular in its fermented/pickled form with salt and water as a condiment. Both fresh and preserved varieties can be found in Asian supermarkets – often the fresh leaves are sold labelled as *gai choi*.

pandan leaves, also called pandanus or screw pine leaves, are long and thin and have a sweet, distinctive fragrance and flavour. They are used in savoury dishes and desserts – the latter for their taste as much as the green colour they impart. Pandan also comes in extract and paste form; look for fresh pandan leaves in Asian greengrocers.

perilla, known as *shiso* in Japanese, is a type of herb belonging to the mint family, and has a wholly distinctive, somewhat perfumed, flavour. It is used primarily raw, either for folding around ingredients like a wrapper, sliced or torn in salads, or as a garnish for Vietnamese and Laotian noodle and simmered dishes. You can find it at Asian greengrocers.

pickled garlic are whole bulbs of garlic, pickled in salt, vinegar and sugar, which are used in Thai and Vietnamese cooking – particularly in central and northern Thai curries, sauces and soups. It's easy to find in Asian supermarkets and keeps for a very long time if refrigerated.

pork floss, also known as *rousong*, is finely shredded, dried pork with a very light and fluffy texture. It is used as a topping for dishes like congee or fried sticky (glutinous) rice, as a filling for pastries or as a snack food. Buy it from Chinese and Asian supermarkets.

prahok is the salted and fermented fish paste used in Cambodian cuisine – it is also used in Laos, where it is known as *padek*. It has a very strong taste and smell so is used sparingly to impart a unique background flavour to all manner of dishes. It needs to be simmered in water and the solids strained before using. In the West, the products available in jars called 'Gouramy Fish Sauce' (made in Thailand), are the closest thing to genuine prahok.

rice paddy herb is native to Southeast Asia and has hints of lemon and cumin. It is used in soups and sauces, especially in Vietnamese cuisine. It can be hard to find, but try Vietnamese or Thai greengrocers. If you can't find it, simply omit it from the recipe.

salted radish, known as *huah chai bpoh* in Thai, is salted and pickled daikon (white radish). The resulting product is both salty and sweet as well as somewhat chewy. It adds textural contrast to curries, noodles, soups and rice dishes. Give it a good rinse before using.

sambal oelek is an extremely spicy Indonesian condiment, traditionally made using a mortar and pestle. Based mainly on pounded red chillies, it features secondary ingredients such as shallots, garlic, shrimp paste, fish sauce, ginger and lime. It is readily available in jars from Asian supermarkets.

saw-tooth coriander, called *pak chi farang* in Thai, owes its common English name to the long, thin serrated edges of the leaves. The herb is extremely fragrant and is used to flavour and garnish all kinds of soups, curries, salads, rice and fish dishes.

shrimp paste is a common ingredient in Southeast Asian cuisine, and comes in many guises, all of them reasonably pungent. Shrimp paste lends a distinctive background flavour to spice pastes and sauces and will last a long time if you keep it refrigerated. As it's quite strong, it is used in small quantities. Belacan is the Malaysian version and is sold in a solid block. Trasi is the name for Indonesian shrimp paste, also sold in a block. Both types are raw and require toasting in foil before using. The Thai version tends to be less solid and is called gapi. It can be used raw, or lightly toasted to enhance its flavour.

snake beans, also known as yard-long or Chinese long beans, are green, long and thin. They are used cooked and raw in curries, stir-fries and salads or as an accompaniment. Buy them from Asian greengrocers.

tamarind pulp is a dark brown, bittersweet pulp that comes from tamarind tree pods, and is used as a souring agent in Southeast Asian cooking. Although you can buy tamarind purée that's ready to go, the flavour is superior when you prepare it yourself, using pieces of thick, sticky pulp. You can buy this as a block from Asian supermarkets, but it needs to be soaked first in boiling water, then strained to remove the seeds and fibre.

tapioca flour, or tapioca starch, is a starchy white flour made from the cassava plant. It is used in a variety of ways, from thickening sauces to baking.

tempeh, also spelled tempe, is a highly nutritious, traditional soy product from Indonesia. It is made by fermenting soy beans and it comes in firm, pressed cakes. It has a nutty flavour and is most commonly cooked by frying. Find it in the refrigerator section of Asian supermarkets.

Thai basil, called *bai horapa* in Thai, is a herb commonly used in Thailand, Vietnam, Cambodia and Laos. It has a marked peppery–licorice flavour. It is mainly used raw to finish off dishes with its fresh colour and strong taste.

tofu skin, also known as dried bean curd or soy bean skin, is actually the skin that forms on soy milk that has been heated. The skin is skimmed off and dried into sheets. Look for packs of pliable squares of tofu skin in Asian and Chinese supermarkets.

Vietnamese mint, also known as *rau ram* and laksa leaf, is a very popular herb throughout Southeast Asia. It has distinctively spicy, peppery notes and is used commonly in salads and on herb plates as an accompaniment to many dishes.

water chestnuts are not a nut but a vegetable, indigenous to Southeast Asia. The flesh is white, juicy and crunchy and remains so even when cooked. It has a very mild flavour and is used more for texture, for example in dumpling fillings.

wing beans are long, pale green beans used extensively throughout Southeast Asia. The beans have distinctively frilly, winged edges and a crunchy texture. Their mild flavour suits being eaten raw or cooked. You will find them fresh at Asian greengrocers.

yellow bean sauce, or yellow soy bean paste, is a fermented preparation made from soy beans; it can be smooth or chunky. The Southeast Asian versions are paler than the Chinese variety, but are quite salty. These bean sauces are used as a condiment and also in soups and dipping sauces.

Index